Beginnings

The very best place to start

Beginnings

The very best place to start

Dedication

For Bethan, Owen and Ffion

*You constantly bring joy to my life
and make me proud to be your father.*

*My prayer is that you will find in these pages
all that I have discovered of the goodness and grace of God
and press on to know Him even more.*

Beginnings **The very best place to start**

Paperback: ISBN: 978-1-915787-02-6

This edition October 2022

Layout and design by the author

Published under Biddles Books.

Distributed from Sulby Close, Spalding.

Typeset in Adobe Caslon 11.5pt/13.5pt.

Other books by the author:
The Bigger they are - the harder they fall. ISBN 978-1-914408-82-3
First published October 2021

Acknowledgements

Once more I acknowledge the men and women who sat under my ministry for 20 years at New Street Baptist Church in St Neots. I am for ever grateful for their willingness to invite me to serve them, and for their faithfulness over the years. They made me dig deeper into the things of God, and in many ways made my ministry, under God, all that it became.

I am also deeply indebted to my father in the things of God. Bishop Kenneth C Ulmer, you continue to challenge me, teach me and correct me. You make me delve into my heart and soul, examine the Scriptures and test my convictions and traditions against the touchstone of the truth of the Word of God. I thank God for you, for your willingness to watch over me, for your ongoing friendship and for some of the insights into the Scripture which find their outworking in these pages.

My grateful thanks also go to Judith for the encouragement and help she has been and is both in my continuing ministry, and in getting this second book corrected and completed. You bless my life. You are my love, my heart beat. I thank God for you.

Unless otherwise mentioned, quotations from the scriptures
are taken from the English Standard Version or the
Authorised Version of the Bible

Contents

Starting at the beginning

"Only in the New Covenant
does the Old unfold,
and hidden lies the
New Covenant within the Old"
Augustine (354-430AD in Dei Verbum)

The Bible is itself a remarkable book. In one sense it is true to say it is made up of 66 books, and yet it is just as true to say it is one book, complete only in it's entirety. It contains one central message, which remains the same from the very first word until the very last one. It is not and cannot ever be true to say that the unchanging God changed His mind part way through the history of the world, and developed a second option, when unexpected events took place. That would be a complete denial of the omniscience of the unchanging and eternal God.

For many, the problem when they come to the Bible, is knowing where to start reading and how to comprehend the various parts, styles and forms of the book.

Many different suggestions are given, and the truth is, where it is best for you to start can depend on your circumstances and situation. If you only have a short time to live, it is probably not the best thing to start by reading Leviticus. On the other hand if you jump right in to the middle of any book, you will quickly find yourself confused, at a loss to fully understand what is going on, or at the very least missing the allusions to earlier parts of the story.

A well known song from a hit musical proclaimed, "Let's start at the very beginning, the very best place to start." Yet that truth, which is reckoned to be the best option in almost every other area of life and study is remarkably overlooked when it comes to opening the Bible. Indeed, even hearing people speak from the Old Testament, within Christian circles tends to be rare, as though the only truth of God is to be found within the New Testament, but when Jesus was ministering on the earth, and when the Church began there were only 39 sacred books of Scripture. Everything taught in that early church was then taught and held to be true, based upon what has become known as the Old Testament.

When Oscar Hammerstein first wrote those words about starting at the beginning, he concluded his wisdom with these last words "If you know the notes to sing, you can sing most anything.".

I therefore invite you to come on a journey with me, in order to look at the first four chapters of the Bible, discovering the notes of God's melody, in His message to the world. I firmly believe, when you start at the beginning and see those first revelations and notes, other portions, which may otherwise seem confusing or strange, will slowly begin to fit into the big picture, and help us find the full wonder of the revelation God chose to give both of Himself and our own condition.

Here in these first chapters of Genesis the foundations and core of the whole message of God is set in place. When those foundations are understood, the reader of the Bible will begin to discover how the rest of the books develop the revelations found at the start.

The first book of the Bible reveals the God who made everything. He reveals Himself then as the God of Abraham, Isaac and Jacob. Later in the Bible He is seen to be not only the God of the Old Testament but also the God and Father of our Lord Jesus Christ. The children of faith, those who believe in the promise of salvation through the shed blood of the Lord Jesus, are throughout the New Testament described as the "children of Abraham", and follow in the line of promise revealed even in the first four chapters of Genesis.

There is not merely a harmony within the Scripture, but a unique close connection in every part, with one grand purpose, carried forward through all the changes of time and history, requiring neither adjustment or variation from beginning to end. The faithfulness, power, perfection and eternal love of the majesty of God is the same in every part. He reveals Himself as true and unchanging on every page. The one purpose of the whole book is to reveal God, and shine a light upon His infinite love for a world He made for Himself, a love which on every page and at every stage of the history recorded within it's pages, is made fully known in the person of Jesus the Christ.

That was the view of Jesus, Himself. It was the view of the early church whose history is recorded in the Book of the Acts, it is the view that undergirds every epistle, and the Apocalypse. It was the view of the early church fathers, yet somewhere, over time, it seems to have been all too forgotten, and has created much of the confusion and error manifest among the people of God today.

Let us change that, come back to the Bible and see again the very beginnings which expound and explain the situation and circumstances around us in the world in which we live.

David S Williams
Spalding.

Beginnings

Beginning to create

In the beginning, God created the heavens and the earth. The earth was without form and void, and darkness was over the face of the deep. And the Spirit of God was hovering over the face of the waters. And God said, "Let there be light," and there was light. And God saw that the light was good. And God separated the light from the darkness. God called the light Day, and the darkness he called Night. And there was evening and there was morning, the first day.

Genesis 1:1-5.

The English Bible in almost every translation begins with the words, "In the beginning God". The words themselves have entered into the very fabric of society and are used and quoted in many different contexts. The only problem is those words can tend to suggest that there was nothing and nobody there before the beginning of verse 1 of Genesis. Such a thought would be quite wrong.

The Bible never speaks of the origin of God, nor does it anywhere seek to prove the existence of God. It understands and accepts that before the beginning began, God was there. Throughout it's pages the Bible holds to the truth revealed succinctly by the writer of the Hebrews; "whoever would draw near to God must believe that He exists and that He rewards those who diligently seek Him."

The original Hebrew of this first verse of Genesis would be better translated 'in the beginning of creating God made...'. The purpose of those first words explain, not the existence of God, but the very nature of the God who was there before

5

the beginning began. They introduce the reader to the creative God who has chosen to reveal Himself and His purposes to the creation He has made by the words which are to follow. He who was before the beginning began, decided to make something called 'the heavens and the earth'. In all that follows those first words, the Maker of it all will set out everything we need to know to discover what He is like and what He desires from the world He has made.

These first words reveal at least two things to the reader of the scriptures. They reveal God as the origin and source of all that there is, and they declare Him to be a God who is actively involved, not passively indifferent when it comes to what He has made.

Then it shows this active God, who is the source of all things, as one who has the ability to make something out of nothing. He is one who does something, in order to change the nothingness into something. This ability to make somethings, out of nothings is an activity God does all by Himself.

He is the only one who alone can take the nothingness we are, and make us into something of His choosing. Every time someone tells us, "we are nothing", or "we will never amount to anything," it places us in the ideal position for God to do and make something worthwhile out of us. He specialises in making somethings out of nothings.

Then the Bible says, the revelation we need to comprehend has to do with God's creating of the 'heavens and the earth'.

When it speaks of the heavens and the earth, we must understand it is not speaking of anything we would immediately recognise as we look around us. There was an earth, but none of the plants or animals we would recognise are necessarily there. He made the heavens, but this is not speaking of the sky which comes later. Nor is the writer referring to the sun, moon and stars, which also come later. He is speaking of something else which is here called 'the earth', and somewhere called 'the heavens'.

The writer says no more about these heavens, beyond the fact that they were made, but turns to draw attention to 'the earth'. By verse 2 we are told this created element called 'the earth' is 'without form', is 'void' and is also covered in darkness. The heavens are not like that, just the earth. There is a difference between the heavens and the earth set out here in this simple statement.

The word which is translated 'without form', is a word which speaks not just of emptiness, but of confusion and chaos. It describes a formless and confused wasteland. The word 'void' is a word which speaks of a superficial indistinguishable ruin. We are then told darkness covers the face of the deep. The word translated 'darkness' is a word which speaks of distress, terror, and evil, of an impenetrable darkness, and the term 'face of the deep' speaks of a 'covering of disturbance and confusion.'

All that means, by verse 2, the earth, though not the heavens can be described as a wasteland of chaotic confusion where everything has been ruined and brought to distress and terror. The whole substance of what is referred to by the term 'earth' is disturbed troubled and dark.

Throughout the whole of the Bible we are presented with God as a being of order. It speaks of the God who is light and who has within Him no darkness at all. It therefore seems inconceivable to describe the work of God as a chaotic, ruin, where there is disturbance and confusion. Something must surely have taken place between verse 1 and verse 2. Something has gone badly wrong, something has brought ruin to the earth, but only to the earth and not the heavens. Whatever has taken place has made the earth a place or terror chaos, destruction and horror.

Alfred Edersheim writes: "An almost indefinite space of time, and many changes, may therefore have intervened between the creation of the heavens and earth, as mentioned in the first verse and the chaotic state of our earth, as described in verse two. As for the exact date of the first creation, it may safely be affirmed that we have not yet the knowledge sufficient to arrive at any really trustworthy conclusion." (Bible History - Vol 1 pp18-19).

What it was like at the first, is impossible to imagine. There are some clues given in different places in the Bible about what may have brought about the change in the earth, from what God must have created at the first and the condition of the earth as it appears in verse two. There are clues in Job, in Ezekiel, in Jeremiah and also from the lips of the Saviour, Jesus the Christ who says He saw 'Satan fall from heaven like lightning'. But while there are clues, they are only clues, but this book of beginnings does tell us, of a world which God made, which by verse 2 has been brought to a state of chaos, trouble, fear and darkness.

By the second verse of this book of beginnings, a kingdom of heaven, and a kingdom of darkness are both being introduced to the reader. The kingdom of darkness is a kingdom of chaos, of terror, of fears and distress.

That kingdom is not going to be left to continue it's reign of terror and chaos unhindered. God is about to intervene, and show Himself as intimately concerned for the world He has made. The very next thing recorded in the second verse introduces the activity of God the Holy Spirit moving across the earth. Where there was darkness, He began to move, to hover, to brood like a mother hen over her young. He began to move over springs of water, over fountains of life giving streams. As the Spirit of God moved gently across the chaotic ruin and darkness, fresh hope and order began to be established.

> *And God said, "Let there be light," and there was light. And God saw that the light was good. And God separated the light from the darkness. God called the light Day, and the darkness he called Night. And there was evening and there was morning, the first day.*

Literally we are told, God spoke. He is a God who speaks. He is a God who reveals Himself by words. Words are revelations of the nature of the one speaking. God is not silent, He speaks, and every time he speaks, He does so to limit and change the dark, the chaotic, the fearful and the wasted. The first thing God speaks is light. He spoke light and light was. In the midst of the darkness God said light be in the midst of the darkness, and light suddenly shone.

By the start of verse 3 the reader is introduced to this God who is active in His creation, who makes somethings from nothings, and is a God who will bring light in order to dispel darkness. The light He often chooses to bring is Himself. He comes Himself, by His Spirit, into the situations and circumstances, for He is light.

As He comes into the darkness and chaos in the world, He turns things around and begins to bring order and hope. This is before the sun, moon or stars are brought into being. But God comes and moves, bringing the light He is. No matter how dark, how chaotic, how distressing a situation may be, this God is always able to turn it around and shine light in a way that dispels the darkness.

God saw the light that it was good. Everything He does and everything He brings is good. He is good and He does good.

Then in verse 4 we are told that God separated the light from the darkness. He set the distinction in place between that which is dark and that which is light. He set out the reality that you will never be able to mix or mingle darkness and light. Light will always dispel darkness. They can never exist together, they can never be joined together. Darkness may seek to obscure or extinguish light, but light will always remove darkness. The two elements and everything those two elements represent will always be opposed to one another, and the overcoming power of light is always assured.

Then in verse 5 it says the evening and the morning were the first day. When it says evening and morning, we need to be careful to understand what it is really saying, because we define evenings and mornings in terms of sunsets and sunrises. But the sun has not been created at this point. The use of the term evening and morning must refer to some time frame, but not necessarily the one we expect.

What we are seeing may more accurately be set out in this way. Since verse 2 when everything was darkness, even though it all appears to be dark, and though it may be black as night at the beginning, the darkness will always be

followed by the rising of light upon the scene.
There is something about the rhythms, the cycles which God works in. There is a rhythm in everything that God makes. There is always a cycle at work. The evening will ever be followed by the morning. That cycle will run right through this first chapter until the seventh day is reached, when God sets down rest as the final act. But that same rhythm will continue to occur throughout the scriptures.

There is something about the way God works. Weeping may endure for the night, but as surely as day follows night, joy will come in the morning. God comes at the very start of the revelation of Himself and shows Himself to be active, and creative, as the one who specialises in turning nothing into something and speaks light into the darkness to create new order and day. No matter how dark and hopeless things appear, He can turn things around. The psalmist declares:

> *You have turned for me my mourning into dancing; you have loosed my sackcloth and clothed me with gladness, that my glory may sing your praise and not be silent. O Lord my God, I will give thanks to you forever!*   *Psalm 30:11-12*

He always brings light to bear on the darkness, joy to replace sorrow, hope to remove despair, life to follow death. It may seem dark, it may appear hopeless, but it is never over until God says so, and while He still reigns, we can always look up in hope and trust. It is this same God who spoke light, and dispelled the darkness that the Apostle Paul speaks of when he declares, writing to the church in Corinth;

> *For God, who said, "Let light shine out of darkness," has shone in our hearts to give the light of the knowledge of the glory of God in the face of Jesus Christ.*   *2 Corinthians 4:6.*

11

It is the reminder that God is light, and He alone is the true light who dispels darkness, chaos, and fear. That light is only truly found in Jesus the Christ, the light of the world.

> *Where there was darkness,*
> *You came and now there's an abundance of light.*
> *Nothing but sinkin' sand*
> *Suddenly I reach out*
> *There's your hand*
>
> *What a feeling it is to know*
> *You're in my corner*
> *And you won't let me go*
> *And now I know that I won't be alone no more*
>
> *I'll give you all I have*
> *And if you teach me I will learn to give you more*
> *You are my anchor now*
> *And like a ship at sea*
> *Ooh, your love will steady me*
>
> *What a feeling this is to know*
> *You're in my corner*
> *And you won't let me go*
> *And now I know that I won't be alone no more*

(©Nickolas Ashford / Valerie Simpson)

The second and third period

And God said, "Let there be an expanse in the midst of the waters, and let it separate the waters from the waters." And God made the expanse and separated the waters that were under the expanse from the waters that were above the expanse. And it was so. And God called the expanse Heaven. And there was evening and there was morning, the second day. And God said, "Let the waters under the heavens be gathered together into one place, and let the dry land appear." And it was so. God called the dry land Earth, and the waters that were gathered together he called Seas. And God saw that it was good. And God said, "Let the earth sprout vegetation, plants yielding seed, and fruit trees bearing fruit in which is their seed, each according to its kind, on the earth." And it was so. The earth brought forth vegetation, plants yielding seed according to their own kinds, and trees bearing fruit in which is their seed, each according to its kind. And God saw that it was good. And there was evening and there was morning, the third day.   *Genesis 1:6-13*

As we come to the record of the second and third periods of time in creation, we are introduced to something the ESV calls 'an expanse', King James calls it 'the firmament', one other translation calls it 'a vault' and one more calls it 'a space'. The word which appears in the Hebrew text is a word which speaks of an extended expanse, of a space between and an extended surface. 'Firmament' is a word which comes into the english language from the latin translation of the Old Testament.

We have no real idea of what the earth would have been like at this stage. All we can tell from these early verses is that the overall impression given would have been of water. Beyond that, we cannot be sure. It is always worth realising, not just what we are told, but what we are not told. The absence of details ought to remind us, that this book is not intended to be either a strict chronological and scientific text book. Instead it's purpose is intended to show us what God is like. The very absence of some details should also impress upon our minds the reality of not needing to know everything. God rarely gives details about how he does things, but about the nature of the 'who' that is involved in the activity.

What we do know from this sixth verse is, God made a space, an extended area around the surface of the earth. You and I refer to it as the atmosphere around our planet. You can see the way that atmosphere extends around the surface, but is also bounded at the extent of it, by taking a high flying aircraft. At 35,000 feet, you can see the curve of the atmosphere holding to the shape of the planet and forming a surface edge. This is what verse six of this amazing chapter tells us God did, and it tells us this fact before anybody could fly and prior to them having the scientific ability to reason out the form of the air we breathe!

Then this sixth verse tells us, having made the space between the surface of the planet and the edge of the atmosphere God said, "let the water be divided. Some to stay locked to the surface of the earth, and some to be held in the expanse above the surface of the planet." God said "I will divide water from water", speaking to a single mass of water and forming it into two bodies of water and instructing part of that water to stay in the space above the earth. It appears at this time, the water in the atmosphere was not held as clouds, but was all held in the air creating a high humidity which would come down as a thick dew every morning. The water in the air was also to be used for the life God was about to bring into being. At every stage He is the author and sustainer of life. At this time God has still not brought sun, moon or stars into being.

In recording the dividing of the waters into two bodies of water and making a difference between them both, God reveals Himself to be the one who can make a division where things look inseparable. It also reminds us that when God separates things, they will remain divided unless and until God brings a reuniting. He is also the one who, in uniting things, makes what can never be divided by any but Him.

The expanse above the earth God called heaven. This word 'heaven' simply means lifted up. So the extended space with this water vapour was to be held up as the atmosphere, and God called it 'lifted up'. This all took place, and evening and morning marked the conclusion of the second period.

It is of interest to discover that the word translated evening, in ancient Hebrew, is a word which speaks of chaos, and this word morning, in ancient Hebrew is a word which speaks of order. If we take the ancient Hebrew the writer has put something like this; then the chaos was invaded a little further by order and a second period passed. It suggests a gradual change. Clearly God could have done it all instantly, but He chooses rather to bring the chaos back into order, little by little. As God, He often chooses to do things in stages, in segments, little by little, from glory to glory.

The coming of light was instantaneous. God said 'light' and light was. But the order which now drives back the chaos, does so step by step. Life comes into being as an immediate response to God speaking, but the establishing of the order and style of the living God is ever a progressive work.

The next words recorded tell us God spoke to the waters covering the earth to gather them into one place in order for dry land to appear, and be seen.

Whether the land was always there, but just covered by the waters, or whether the gathering of the waters was concurrent with the appearing of the earth, we are not told. It is possible God gathered the waters and called the dry land into being at the same time, it is equally possible that he called the waters together, in order for that which was not seen, to become evident. Neither are we told what the substance and form of the earth was, prior to it becoming waste and desolate.

It is worth realising, that when we come honestly and without preconception to these verses, we are left with many questions which will stay unanswered. What we can say without any doubt is, the earth we now look upon, has not always been as we see it today. It is the Apostle Peter who picks this thought up as he writes to all those who have a faith of equal standing with his by the righteousness of our God and Savior Jesus Christ. He says there are many who question the truths of the gospel and doubt the faithfulness of God to His word. They call in to question God's declaration to replace all we now see with a new heaven and earth. They doubt that intention because they assume that everything is as it always has been. He declares such people are willingly ignorant, and deliberately overlook this fact;

> *the heavens existed long ago, and the earth was formed out of water and through water by the word of God.*   *2 Peter 3:5*

Once God called the waters; sea and the dry land; earth He again looked at what had been achieved and declared it to be good. Bringing further order out of the chaos.

Having brought the dry land into being God speaks and gives instruction to the earth that it should now bring forth. The ESV does not sufficiently show the Hebrew forms of plant life which is described here. In saying *'vegetation'*, *'plants'* and *'trees'* three different forms of vegetation are described in the original. They speak of the dry land bringing forth, grasses, herbs and trees into being.

Once again there are details which we are not told. Did they come forth as elements already grown and with age, or did they come as shoots across the earth? We do not know and need not speculate. It is unimportant how it looked as each of the three came forth. All we need to understand here is that there were three different forms of vegetation, a threefold variety of greenery which came forth. But all three have one thing in common, and in case you miss it, it is expressly repeated in the verses.

Twice, it says, each form of vegetation has seed within it and that each seed, in each type, is seed only of its own form of greenery. That is to say the seed in the grass, will never produce trees. But each of the three forms of greenery have life within the seed. Seed which is able to reproduce it's own form of life. There in verse 11-12 we are being introduced to the purpose and value of seed.

We are shown three important elements to the value of seed. First, we are shown that every element of the created life being brought forth, has seed within it, which will be the means of spreading and filling the earth with life. This word for seed speaks specifically of descendents, of producing more. Seed speaks of flourishing and increasing. It speaks of abundance and fruitfulness.

Every seed has the ability to reproduce one of its own kind. But each one of its own kind has the ability to reproduce more than one seed. It means that each seed has within it an almost limitless ability to produce more of its own. God is a God who creates things which have the capacity for fruitful abundance.

The second thing that seed speaks of has to do with death, and that is especially interesting to notice because it comes before the fall, before the sin of Adam and Eve. The seed speaks of new life, coming and flowing out from death. Unless a seed falls into the ground and dies, it abides alone, but if it dies it brings forth much fruit.

Then the third thing being introduced here is the reality that a seed will only produce more of the same thing from which it came. That speaks of the variety which God made. He is a God of variety, but it also brings an incredible truth to bear. However often you plant grass seed, it will never produce an apple tree, and however regularly you plant plum stones, they will never create a good crop of barley.

Even writing that seems ridiculously obvious, and yet we are told that everything around us has evolved from some simple cell organism. Back here at the very start, the very absurdity of that idea is set out, and the more science discovers about the DNA of different species the more ridiculous it seems to appear. God made some grasses, some herbs and some trees.

Finally a creation ordinance which holds true in every area

of the creation is being set out here. What you sow will always determine what you reap and what you reap will always be a manifestation of what you have sown. It is in the very nature of seed, to produce it's own.

We must always realise that if what we are doing in any area of life is not working for us, it is just plain foolish to keep on doing the same thing in the hope that the result will change. If we keep doing the same thing, it will always produce the same result. We need to understand this truth about seed. In order to obtain a different result in any area of life, requires us to do something different first. Only when we change the nature of what we are sowing will we ever see the desire to reap a different result being fulfilled.

This truth ends the third period of bringing order into the chaos the enemy of souls had brought to pass on this earth.

\

The fourth and fifth period

And God said, "Let there be lights in the expanse of the heavens to separate the day from the night. And let them be for signs and for seasons, and for days and years, and let them be lights in the expanse of the heavens to give light upon the earth." And it was so. And God made the two great lights—the greater light to rule the day and the lesser light to rule the night—and the stars. And God set them in the expanse of the heavens to give light on the earth, to rule over the day and over the night, and to separate the light from the darkness. And God saw that it was good. And there was evening and there was morning, the fourth day.

And God said, "Let the waters swarm with swarms of living creatures, and let birds fly above the earth across the expanse of the heavens." So God created the great sea creatures and every living creature that moves, with which the waters swarm, according to their kinds, and every winged bird according to its kind. And God saw that it was good. And God blessed them, saying, "Be fruitful and multiply and fill the waters in the seas, and let birds multiply on the earth." And there was evening and there was morning, the fifth day.   *Genesis 1:14-23*

By the end of the third period, God has moved sufficiently to ensure all things needful for the sustaining of life are in place, yet as he turns to the fourth period of bringing order into the chaos, He does something remarkable, for He sets in place sources of light in the expanse of the heavens. Lights to divide day and night. He speaks light bearing objects into being. The God who is light, in and of Himself, now chooses to create objects to bear light into the world He has made.

Nothing that God ever makes or does, is without purpose. All that He ever does has a purpose and all that He ever brings into being is brought forth to fulfil the purpose He designed and created it for.

When it comes to these lights in the firmament He tells us His purpose in creating them is to give signs, seasons, days and years. God declares these bodies of light have three objectives. They are created to be signs, they are there to set seasons and then by their very existence they will mark days and years. Those are three very separate and distinct purposes.

God's first reason for setting the sun, the moon and the stars in place was that they should be signs. The great light, the sun is a sign in the daytime. The moon and the stars are to be a sign in the night time. They are all there to signify something, and they signify this at different times and in different ways. Signs are objects used to communicate a message. There are several messages which can be noticed by meditating on the signs of the sun moon and stars.

It is clear that between the sun, moon and stars there was never to be a moment when light failed to shine upon this world. There may be times when the light is diminished or obscured by the clouds or the particular topography of certain places, but, even when you cannot see them, they are still shining a light into the darkness. No matter how dark, how dismal how black things appear, the blackness of the darkness cannot extinguish the shining of the light, all it can ever do is obscure or hide the reality of the light that still shines. The darkness can never overcome the light. So the songwriter declares:

> *In the midst of the darkness*
> *You're the light that guides me through*
> *Our eyes are on You*
> *You are near to the broken*
> *The weak find their strength in You*
> *Our eyes are on You*
>
> *We lift our eyes to You where our help comes from*
> *Our hope is found in You Jesus, Lord of all*
> *We lift our eyes to You Exalted One.*
> *(©Elevation Worship)*

They are there as signs, as direction for the path we need to take as we navigate our way through life. People have long since learned to navigate their journey and check their direction by means of the light which comes from these heavenly bodies. God has put these light bearers into the world in order for humanity to best determine the safe direction of travel and the correct path to take in life. So the psalmist declares:

> *Your word is a lamp to my feet and a light to my*
> *path.*   *Psalm 119:105*

Then we discover that the lesser light is in truth, only a reflection of the greater light. It is the reflection of the greater light created to shine into the darkness of the night season. It is no mystery that He who declared Himself to be the light of the world, then turned to those who followed Him and said "you are the light of the world", not that they were light in themselves, but that they were to reflect the light of the glory of God, by their relationship with Jesus the Christ.

These heavenly bodies are also there for seasons. When we read that english word, we have a tendency to think only in terms of the four seasons of the year, but the Hebrew word used speaks rather of 'fixed times'. It speaks of a God who has set in place times for different things, for different periods, for different eras. As each begins, we can often think the season we are in will last for ever. God chooses here to declare the truth that everything has it's season, and that seasons come and go, with every season having a limit set by the God who reigns supreme in the heavens.

Actually this word translated 'seasons' has the idea of an 'appointed fixed time'. It is a reminder that God knows the beginning from the end. He sets the start and He determines the conclusion of all things. Jesus said that it was not for us to know the times and the seasons, but God knows them all. The fixed length of the period for everything is determined by the Sovereign God. He even sets the day I came forth and the day this body will return to the dust.

Then God reminds us they are also there to be the means of measuring periods and time, the length of days, years and eras. They are there to remind us of the passing of time, to remind us that time marches on and stops for none but God.

God made the sun and the moon and the stars also. Then the writer adds these two great lights were there not just for those three purposes but they are also given a defined function. The great and the lesser light were to rule the day and the night.

In the english versions, we are told twice that the sun and the moon are there to rule. In verse 16 and again in verse 18 the word rule is used, but in the original there are two different words used. The first word speaks of ruling by taking dominion over the day and the night. They are there to control and to dominate the two different periods governing them and keeping them within their own bounds. The second word also speaks of this authority to rule and reign, to govern and take dominion, but it has the additional note that this is a delegated authority. They tell us these bodies were created with the authority to rule but only as far as it had been delegated to them and for the time that was predetermined by the one who has the overall right to rule and reign.

That is a concept which will be found elsewhere in this narrative, for the Sovereign Lord alone has absolute authority to reign supreme, but He chooses to delegate that authority at times, into the hands of various parts of His creation. Here, for a while, he delegates the bringing of light into the darkness of the globe to these two celestial bodies. He takes the authority, which is His alone, and delegates it in order for them to obey what He has said, and perform the purpose for which they have been created. Obedience on their part gives an insight into the purpose of delegating authority to them. Every day time and night time, the sun and the moon act in absolute obedience to the delegated authority which God has placed upon them.

God looked at this response of obedience, and the further driving back of the chaos and blackness, and once more declares this new step to be good.

On the fifth day God spoke to the waters. It is interesting to note that sometimes He spoke to nothing to make something, but at other times He chose to speak to something to bring forth new life. So it was that He spoke to the earth, to create the vegetation. Now He speaks to the waters to bring forth living creatures.

That word requires the waters to bring forth two completely distinct kinds of creatures. There are to be those which are to fill the sky and are capable of flight, and those which fill the waters, which also have this ability to move from place to place. These are to be creatures that move through the air, and through the waters. It is very different to the creation of vegetation, this is the creation of species with the ability to move at their own volition.

We must notice the word 'swarm' or 'abundant'. The word used in the original speaks of a vast array. What God is doing is not on the small scale, it is a multitude, a teeming mass, an abundant swarm of all these different creatures. He is a God of abundance.

But He is also a God of variety. Twice in the twenty first verse the phrase "according to it's kind" appears. That phrase is the translator's attempt at a word which speaks of species, or of kinds. It is a reminder that God is not bound by a single option but loves diversity. It also reminds us that creatures that fly and creatures that live in the water are not from the same stock. This one word 'kind' is defined in the NAS Hebrew Lexicon in this way:

> Groups of living organisms belong in the same created kind is they have descended from the same ancestral pool. This does not preclude new species, because this represents a partitioning of the original gene pool. Information is lost or conserved and not gained. A new species could arise where a population is isolated and inbreeding occurs. By this definition a new species is not a new kind but a further partitioning of an existing kind.

As the waters are swarming with life and the sky is filled with living creatures God stops and once more looks at the effect of driving back the dark chaos, and declares "this is good".

The twenty second verse introduces a further new concept of the plan and purpose of the living God. He looks at the creatures which are in the sea and in the sky and speaks directly to them.

This is the first time that God speaks to what He has made, as soon as He has brought it into being. It is also the first time He speaks to what He has created with an instruction for their own existence. He has previously spoken to both the earth and the waters and told them to bring forth something different. He has also spoken to the waters to do things to move to govern the extent of their reach, but now He speaks to these living creatures with a word which is just for them and their existence.

The very first thing God says to living creatures, the very first word He has for them, is a word of blessing. The word of God stands secure and He watches over it to bring it to pass. His first word to any living creatures, the first thing He wants to impart, is a word of blessing. To bless is to wish, and in the case of God it is to will, some good to the object of blessing. Before He even creates mankind He says His will, His heart's desire is to see good come upon His creation.

The nature of the blessing is remarkable. The very first blessing God pronounces within this book of beginnings is a threefold blessing. It is a blessing to be fruitful, to multiply and to fill the areas allotted to them.

The first word translated 'fruitful' speaks of multiplying increase. It is a blessing for them to become more numerous than they were at the beginning. The second word translated 'multiply' is a word which speaks of prospering and enlarging growth. To prosper means 'to go well', and enlarge the area of influence and the boundaries of existence. The final word 'fill' is a word which speaks of accomplishing and fulfilling the purpose which has been allocated to them.

From the very beginning, lack, extinction, reduction, maintaining were never in the plan of God for His creation. They are all words which speak of the plan and purpose of the evil one, who comes to steal, kill and destroy. God's plan and purpose is ever for His creation to increase numerically, to increase the area of their influence, and fulfil every purpose and plan for which it was brought into being. It was this from the first creation, and it is the same for the new creation in Christ Jesus.

It is why Jabez would later pray:
> *"Oh that you would bless me and enlarge my border, and that your hand might be with me, and that you would keep me from harm so that it might not bring me pain!" And God granted what he asked.*   *1 Chronicles 4:10*

With these words of blessing pronounced on the creatures of the air and sea, the chaos and darkness is driven still further back and the fifth period has come to an end.

The sixth period

And God said, "Let the earth bring forth living creatures according to their kinds—livestock and creeping things and beasts of the earth according to their kinds." And it was so. And God made the beasts of the earth according to their kinds and the livestock according to their kinds, and everything that creeps on the ground according to its kind. And God saw that it was good. Then God said, "Let us make man in our image, after our likeness. And let them have dominion over the fish of the sea and over the birds of the heavens and over the livestock and over all the earth and over every creeping thing that creeps on the earth." So God created man in his own image, in the image of God he created him; male and female he created them. And God blessed them. And God said to them, "Be fruitful and multiply and fill the earth and subdue it, and have dominion over the fish of the sea and over the birds of the heavens and over every living thing that moves on the earth." And God said, "Behold, I have given you every plant yielding seed that is on the face of all the earth, and every tree with seed in its fruit. You shall have them for food. And to every beast of the earth and to every bird of the heavens and to everything that creeps on the earth, everything that has the breath of life, I have given every green plant for food." And it was so. And God saw everything that he had made, and behold, it was very good. And there was evening and there was morning, the sixth day.   *Genesis 1:24-31*

So much has already been revealed in the first twenty three verses of the nature and being of God, of His interest and relationship to His creation. As we reach the sixth period the world is beginning to look almost recognisable to the way we see it, though there are still some seismic changes which will take place before it becomes the kind of world in which we dwell. The sky is in place, the earth has a coastline where the sea is held back, the sun moon and stars are in the heavens, vegetation is covering the earth and there are creatures both in the sea and in the air; flying and water bound life is in place and beginning to expand to populate the space assigned to them by God.

At the commencement of the sixth period, God speaks once more to the earth, this time giving it instruction to bring forth living creatures, some of which will crawl and creep across the earth, some to be good as livestock, and yet more variety to make every other kind of land based creature. Once again God says they are to be brought forth after their kind. The Hebrew word is the same as we noticed in the last chapter, with the same restrictions, that each species will only produce after their own kind. A spider will never evolve into a donkey, and probably only a donkey could imagine such a thing could be possible.

Once more God looks at what has been produced by His word and declares it to all be good.

Within the first chapter of Genesis, and over the six periods so far considered a kind of formula has been in place. Everything has begun with an announcement, "And God said". This has been followed by a command "bring forth". There is next a report following the command, "and it was so". This is followed with an evaluation of the response to the command of God "God saw it was good". Finally there is a period or time frame of 'evening followed by morning'.

In following through that very deliberate sequence of events we can see a very clear revelation from God. It is clear that everything God says, then takes place. It is also noticeable that whatever God speaks to, immediately responds in obedience to His word. Notice also that obedience to God's command always brings about a clear and good result and that God evaluates the obedience as good.

Everything has followed that same formula and brought about the same result until we reach verse twenty six where there is suddenly a complete change to that formula and method. From verse two up to this point God has spoken to something, in order to bring something new into being. This is not the case as we reach this most significant step in the creation narrative. No longer does God speak to something, rather, He now speaks to Himself. Mankind does not come forth as the work of the earth or of the waters bringing forth this new creature, instead mankind comes forth when God speaks to Himself about a desire to make man.

God speaks to Himself in order to give us a new revelation not just of Himself, but also of the value He places on humanity. Nor is it just about humanity as a species. It is a revelation of the value God places on every human being, on every individual, on you and me. It declares rather than making us from nothing, He spoke to Himself, calling us into being from His own essence, and when He made us, He placed into us and stamped on our very being, something of His image. He does all this differently to everything else recorded here, in order that we may realise and never forget the value of who we are and what He made us to be.

31

In this 26th verse there is a revelation of the very nature and essence of God Himself. For this one God, in this first chapter of His revelation, makes an amazing statement about Himself, for as He speaks to Himself, He speaks using a mixture of singular and plural terms. He says, 'Let us make man in our one and only unique image.' It is a revelation of the God who is one God, in more than one persons.

This description of the creation of man as being in the image of God, has caused a large amount of debate over the years as men have sought to discover exactly what is meant by the phrase. Some draw a distinction at this point between the body and the soul or spirit of a human being. But that seems only possible if we add something extraneous to the revelation given in these words.

The straightforward reading of the text would suggest that God, in creating man, made mankind out of his own essence, in a way which means when you looked at man, God intended us to be reminded of Himself. There was to be something about mankind which reminded the whole of creation not only of the gifts to be deposited on mankind; but also something of the very nature and being of God.

The idea of you and me bearing the image of God, which so many struggle with at this point of the text is, in fact, a wholly biblical teaching.

If we turn to the New Testament we discover salvation is meant to return us to a place where we bear the likeness of God. We are to be forgiven and cleansed, but also to be restored in order to bear again the image of God within the world where we exist. We are to be 'conformed to the image of his Son'; conformed to the 'icon' of God's Son.

The word icon, so often used is an interesting word. I used to think an icon spoke about a painting or an object which was worshipped in some expressions of christianity. But I discovered it is not so much an object of worship as a revelation which leads to worship. An icon is a picture that tells a story, and by telling the story means to bring us to a place where we see and worship the activity of the living God in the lives of men and women.

When God made mankind He made us to be a revelation of what He was like and what His purposes were. That does not mean, and never can mean, that you and I are the same as God, but, at the very least, it does mean we were made to be a picture of what God was like in certain aspects. That image, which we will discover was so badly marred in the narrative of Genesis 3 is the image which is ultimately restored in the outcome of the Gospel.

When Jesus dies upon the cross for your sin and mine, it was not just to win our salvation in terms of mere forgiveness, wonderful as that is, it was to restore everything which the devil had stolen and everything that had been marred and lost in Adam. Once we become children of God, we struggle and grapple daily with what it means, for us to be the reflection, the revelation of God, in this world. It is why the phrase is used here at the beginning of human history. It is there to help us realise that bearing the image of God was always His plan. It's presence there also helps us recognise the devastating effects of the unfolding story.

Paul writing to New Testament believers in Ephesus writes that the effect of the Gospel is to make you and me, once more created after God in righteousness and true holiness. In the image of God, the reflection of God's righteousness and holiness.

> *be renewed in the spirit of your minds, and to put*
> *on the new self, created after the likeness of God*
> *in true righteousness and holiness.*
>
> *Ephesians 4:23-24*

The word used there and translated 'holiness' speaks of only doing what is sanctioned by the Lord and being what the Lord desires. The word 'righteousness' used here speaks of only doing what is approved by God as good, and of recognising Him as the judge whose sole approval alone we seek. We were made to do what God said and live to please Him, in a way which reflected His will and His purpose without question, even as Jesus lived. He only did what the Father asked, and only spoke the words His father gave Him.

Understand, when God made man and woman, He made them with the ability to do all He said and all He asked. He gave them the ability to walk in obedience, to walk in righteousness and holiness, to walk in a way which would fully reflect the beauty and glory of the living God.

God goes further than just saying let us make man in our image, he then defines what the role of mankind is to be, as it reflects the nature of the living God. He says man is to have dominion, they are to be in charge and govern every other living creature that God has made, to take authority over them all, and bear a responsibility for all of them.

God having spoken to Himself, then does what He has spoken to Himself and makes mankind, male and female, He created them. A fuller description of all that is involved here is given in Genesis 2 and we will notice some of those further details later in this book.

After God had made humanity, male and female, men and women, both of them, then God spoke to them, to both of them. There is no other way of reading this honestly, and dealing with the text in integrity. God is about to speak to the man and the woman together.

In case we miss that, twice in these first words God speaks to Adam and Eve. We are reminded He is speaking to more than just the man. He says, you both have a role, you both are here for a purpose, you both are to reflect the likeness of the living God and fulfil His will and His purpose in a way which gains His approval. You are both here to live in a way which flows from a desire to see the will of God, brought to bear on earth, even as it is in heaven!

Now be careful, or you will miss something really significant. God speaks all these words to the man and the woman. They both have this blessing and this word spoken over their lives. God did not just speak to man and leave the woman to tag along. The revelation of speaking to both of them together is a reminder of the will and purpose of God, for people to walk into His blessing, together with another. The purpose of God is for us to walk together with another, to be in community, never to walk alone, never to be an island apart. He spoke to both of them, together.

The very first thing God speaks to the man and the woman together is spoken to bless them. Having already blessed them with the ability to live and please God, to reflect the wonder of God in His plans and purposes, He further blesses them with words spoken over them both. God says Be 'fruitful', which is a word meaning 'flourish and increase', and 'multiply' which speaks of knowing increase, and 'replenish the earth' or 'fill the earth'.

God's plan over and over is to start with little and make it increase, to take mustard seeds and fill the earth.

Then God adds 'and subdue it'. Here God instructs the man and the woman to ensure there is nothing anywhere on this earth which they do not bring under their authority and control. God says, this is my blessing, my desire for you, that you will always be the head and never the tail, that you will bring everything under your control and power, as you live your life being a reflection of my will and purpose. It is a clue, that as yet, not everything in the earth was perfect and living under the control of God.

Then God adds, "and govern the animals, the birds and the fish. You are to be their rulers, and never the other way around. You are to govern them, not let them govern you." Then He adds, "and know that the purpose behind every living herb and tree is to provide for your nourishment and the nourishment of all the animals, birds and fish, which you are to govern here on this earth." Man and woman were to live with this delegated authority to be stewards of all that God had made, bringing everything on the earth into submission to the will and purpose of the Almighty.

God looked and said, if all that I have made, lives and does all that I have said the result is not just good, it can already be seen as very good. With that assesment of the situation on the earth, the sixth period ends.

Then there was rest

Thus the heavens and the earth were finished, and all the host of them. And on the seventh day God finished his work that he had done, and he rested on the seventh day from all his work that he had done. So God blessed the seventh day and made it holy, because on it God rested from all his work that he had done in creation. Genesis 2:1–3

At the start of the second chapter of this book of beginnings of the revelation of the living God there is a very real sense that what has been done in chapter one has come to a kind of conclusion. The whole of chapter one has revealed something about the nature of God. It has set the scene for the rest of the Bible. It has revealed a God who is good, a God who is light, a God who is truth, a God who is able to do all He desires and a God who none can stop from working to His time or to His plan. It has revealed a God who is not only good in Himself, but a God who desires good to come upon the world He has made. It has manifested the plan of God to create and then delegate power and authority to his creation, and has placed within that creation the ability to act in accordance with His will and His purpose.

When you turn to the second chapter, the purpose of the revelation moves from concentrating on the nature and being of the living God, to the revelation of God's plan for the world He has made.

So this second chapter begins in this way:
Thus the heavens and the earth were finished, and all the host of them.

It says the heavens and the earth were finished, not that they were perfect, but that the work of making them was now accomplished. It suggests the scene has now been set for what is to come. Not only are the heavens and the earth finished but the whole host of them is now ready for what is to follow.

This term the 'whole host' is a translation of a really interesting word. It speaks of a vast army. The Hebrew word is one which in it's plural form has made it into the English language. It is the word Sabaoth. We sometimes speak of God as the 'Lord of Sabaoth'. Usually the message translation helpfully translates that phrase as "the God of the angel armies". Other translations use the phrase "the Lord of hosts." It speaks of God as the God of the angels, but it also speaks of Him as the one who made and is in charge of the universe, of the constellations, of the stars, and there are a host of them. It speaks of an ordered and organised multitude, of the vastness of their array, beauty, order and splendour.

The next words in this Genesis account declares that once the vast array of all of creation had been brought into being;
> *on the seventh day God finished his work that he had done, and he rested on the seventh day from all his work that he had done.*

Now as this seventh period arrives and the first six periods have passed, God declares that He has come to the end of all He needed to do at this point, in order to bring His purposes to pass, so He now declares it is time to rest, to pause from His creating activity. He sets in place a day of rest.

When it says that God rested, we need to remind ourselves this does not mean he was weary and tired. You and I get weary and worn. He is never weary. He never tires. Nor does it intend us to think He needed to sleep. He never slumbers and never sleeps. He is the God who watches over His creation all the time and throughout all times. Neither should we be tempted to think that at this point God has lost interest in what He had made. It is not as though He made all things and then withdrew to leave the world to get on with things in His absence. He was still actively sustaining the whole of creation. The eyes of all He had made were still upon Him. He was still ensuring everything was working to His scheme, His order and His plan. He did not rest in that sense, but He did set a day of rest as a seventh day.

The plan that He has followed, the way that He has done things is changing at this moment. At the end of every other day, He has made an assessment. On this seventh day He does not make an assessment. Everything He is going to make is already in place. It is that idea of creating which He now rests from. When it says He rested, it speaks of pausing. He paused not to see what was going on but because much of what had been chaos and darkness has now come into order. It has come into light sufficiently for Him to pause.

In resting, He does more than just pause. There are two further things He is about to do on this seventh day.

In pausing, in resting, He sets in place a pattern for His world. That pattern for the whole of creation was to help us to understand that pausing is important. After six periods there is to be a seventh period to pause.

Apart from anything else that pause is there to remind us that God is setting in place the reality that everything within His creation will run for a certain period of time, through a range of periods, and then at the conclusion there will be a rest. The norm which He sets in place is a six period followed by a seventh of rest. Six periods, we might do a range of things, but on the seventh period, we are to do something different, because God says, I made things for six days, but on the seventh I stopped. He sets that down an example for us, so we might understand there is a cycle, a rhythm to life. After six days, there is a seventh day and on the seventh day, God says we are to rest. We are to pause from the activities of the previous six days.

The cycle He put in place has value for us that there might be a rhythm to our life and to our existence. One of the problems for some of us is that every day is in danger of looking and being the same. God says, we need to understand we are meant to live life in the cycle and the rhythm He sets down. This is to be a formula for life.

In pausing from the activity of creation God still was active and that activity included blessing this seventh day. He put a special blessing upon this period of rest.

God comes and says that if we will rest, we will find this day of rest is a day that is particularly blessed. We will find this day is a blessing to us. God comes and explains that if we do not rest and do not change what we are doing we will miss something of the blessing and favour He intends for us.

He blessed the day and set in place this rhythm for life to help us understand that we are intended to live our lives in the rhythm of our relationship with a living God and that when we live life in the rhythms of that relationship our life will increase in blessing.

God then did something further. This seventh day which He

blessed, He then made holy. He sanctified this day of rest.

He did not rest because He was tired, nor did He rest because He couldn't think of anything else to do, He rested in order to instigate and release into the earth realm a divine principle of blessing and holiness.

God comes and says He has blessed this seventh day and made it a holy day. This day of rest is set forth to be a day of knowing God's blessing and honouring it as a special day, a holy day. The whole creation is intended to see and recognise rest that is blessed and rest that is holy.

This word translated 'holy' or in some versions 'sanctified' is a word which speaks of consecration. God sets this day as a day to be set apart, so that all which takes place within it might be consecrated or dedicated to the God of creation.

I struggle with the world I live in. I'm old enough to remember when Sunday saw few, if any, shops open where I was brought up. Today, the towns and shopping malls are filled with crowds coming not to dedicate the day to the God of creation or to bow in worship before Him, but to spend yet more time in shopping. An activity so many seem unable to live without. What it is about shops that having wandered around every other day of the week still draws us back to do the same on this seventh day. I know this, if we do not change our activity on this seventh day in a way which consecrates one period in seven to the living God we will never be as happy and blessed as God desired or intended us to be.

In April 2018 the 'ToysRUs' chain in the UK, which had once claimed to be the biggest and the greatest toy store anywhere in the world, and claimed it would never close down, finally closed their last store. The greatly promoted toy store has gone. They issued various reasons and excuses for their failure. They claimed it was not possible to make money just selling toys.

At the same time, 'The Entertainer' chain of toy stores, which started with just one shop had 145 shops open and was looking to open more. In 2021, even through the pandemic, they are still trading and growing their business. They sell the same range as 'ToyRUs' did, but they performed better. Looking on their website, allows us to discover 'their reasoning for success'. They choose to run their lives and business based on the principles of the living God. On Sunday, their stores are closed, and they claim to run as an ethical business. I find that truly interesting.

Remember this verse in Genesis is not talking specifically about Sunday, which is not the seventh day of the week anyway. I would suggest it does not really matter if we make the day of rest, blessing and consecration Saturday, Sunday, Monday, Tuesday, Wednesday, Thursday, or Friday. When visiting and teaching in Kuwait they gather to rest and consecrate Friday. The name of the day is not significant, the principle is of one day in seven. That one day is the issue. God says, make one in seven a day to consecrate entirely to Him.

We make one day holy, set apart to God. It is a day for worship. It is a day to increase and bless our relationship with this living God, and to be with his people.

Interestingly, the word Sabbath is just another word for seventh. In Exodus 20 God gives to Moses, for the benefit of the people of Israel laws which we have come to call the 10 commandments.

When you get down to commandment number four, God says, 'remember the Sabbath day'. Notice what He does not say. He does not declare the institution of the seventh day. He already did that all the way back in Genesis. He is telling His people to remember. He is reminding us what He set in place in creation, and says, 'remember the Sabbath day to keep it holy, because for six days, the Lord worked and on the seventh, he rested. It is a creation ordinance.

The Apostle James writing says:
> *For whoever keeps the whole law but fails in one*
> *point has become guilty of all of it.   James 2:10*

Now he uses a word in Greek which is translated as 'all'. It is an interesting word, it is a technical word. It means 'ALL'.In Exodus God comes and says, 'remember the Seventh day to keep it holy', remember the creation ordinance which set this day as the day of blessing and consecration. I suggest that commandment is more broken than any other command in our world and in our churches, and James suggests, in breaking this one we are guilty of going against all that God has assigned for us to live by.

God makes a significant point in Exodus 20. Many of the commandments God simply declares, 'You shall do this' or 'You shall not do this'. But when it comes to remembering the seventh day and consecrating it, He takes three verses to explains what it means to keep the day holy in our own lives and in the lives of those we relate to. Because this day is a special day, all the way through the scriptures, God declares that if we will keep this day special, we will be blessed.

There was a day when the Jesus the Christ rode into town, sitting on a donkey. It was a Sunday. We remember it as Palm

Sunday. Then He worked on the Monday. He turned the temple out. He worked on the Tuesday. He worked on the Wednesday. He worked on the Thursday and on the Friday He did the greatest work He ever did. For on that Friday, He died upon a cross for our sin. On the Friday, he took away our curse and accomplished our complete salvation.

After He hung and died upon the cross all day Friday, they came to take the body down. They had to do that before sunset, because in Hebrew culture, sundown is the start of a new day, and the day about to dawn, was the seventh day, a holy day.

At the start of the seventh day, Jesus already had to be in a borrowed tomb because the seventh day is a day of rest. It was a borrowed tomb because He did not need it for long! They laid His body in a borrowed tomb and all day on the seventh day He rested.

Having rested on the seventh day, early the following morning He rose up with all power and authority in heaven and earth, the risen Christ. Only when we rest on the seventh day in the presence of God under the blessing of God, will we ever rise up on the first day with the power we need to live the life God designed for us.

We live in a world where people are walking in stress, depression, misery, struggles. I just wonder when did they last rest and consecrate their rest to God? When did they set aside one day to worship with His people. We worship in order to experience the blessing set upon the seventh day?

There is a word of caution we must be aware of. I remember days when the whole of Sunday was a weariness running from one meeting to the next. I am not saying we need to be in church all day. I am just suggesting the whole day should be set apart and consecrated to God, a day when we pause from all that we do every other day of the week and live to build our relationship with the ever living God?

We need a break. Six days. We need to be blessed. We need to consecrate one day to our relationship with God and to spend it in worship. The devil will try to trick us, cheat us and keep us from the worship of God. He will seek to fill our life with things aimed at keeping us so busy we think we have no time to spare to consecrate a whole day to God. If we listen to the devil, he will seek to steal our relationship and blessing, kill our spiritual life and destroy what God has put in place to bless and prosper us.

God put in place this provision of a day of rest in place for our physical health, our mental health and our spiritual health. We need to rest, we need to know God's blessing and we need to worship.

God comes and declares, this day to be a day of pause, a day of blessing, a day of consecration, the heavens and the earth are ready for the next part of the story. The scene is set for the revelation of God's plans for this world.

Man and woman

The whole of the creation is now ready for the unfolding of the story of God's plan and purpose. Seven periods have passed. Those seven have been told in the manner of an outline, following a formula, which God used to make everything.

From the start of verse four of the second chapter of Genesis we are given another and seemingly different view of the creation narrative.

There are a number of different ways of viewing this second creation narrative. There are some who suggest this chapter covers exactly the same story, but in greater detail. It is certainly true, there are details here which are not included in chapter one. But in chapter one, there are many details which are omitted in chapter two. There are others who say the first chapter is a kind of outline and now there are certain parts of that outline given some further detail.

Instead of either of those theories, I want to suggest chapter one was written with one purpose in mind, while chapter two from verse 5 is written with a very different style, because God has a different purpose in the mind here. This second chapter of Genesis is no longer concerned with the order of the creation of things, nor of the timing of the creation of things. Neither is the writer concentrating any more on the way God pushed back the chaos and darkness to re-establish order and light. Instead, I suggest in this second chapter the writer is concerned to begin to reveal the plan and purpose of God for the creation which He has made.

It means that there is a very real sense of God moving into

the background of the unfolding story as He begins to reveal His plan and purpose for creation, and especially where that purpose has to do with mankind, and the establishment of families and family life.

It is one of those startling things which very few comment on, but God's whole revelation, from this point onwards, has to do with family. His plan, and His purpose for the world is centred around the family. Indeed his plan and His purpose for the new world at the end of time is also revealed to be about family.

God chooses to work in families. As the story proceeds the first family is revealed and God begins to establish and teach lessons about families. It is also important to realise that from the very start, the family God created was not a perfect family. In certain important areas, God chose to make a family with flaws.

The first family God made had issues. Even before the fall, while the creation was good, not everything was perfect and complete. There are some who believe and suggest, if only we could get back to the time in Genesis before the fall of man took place, everything would be wonderful. I suggest that is a wrong reading of these verses and a misunderstanding in interpretation.

God is not going to restore everything back to exactly the same world which existed at the start of this second chapter. Here in chapter two, the devil is around and roaming free upon the earth. When God makes a new heaven and a new earth, it will be a place in which only righteousness dwells.

Not only was the devil there at the start of chapter two, but there were flaws areas God included when He created man. The man He made had something within the creation which God intentionally made and declared 'not good'. He did it for His own purpose and so that mankind would learn lessons about the limitations of isolation and the need for relationship and family.

The flaws we find revealed both before and after the fall of mankind help us to read these verses and feel at one with the story, since we all come to the scripture as people with flaws, limitations, imperfections, struggles and brokenness.

The truth that we find revealed in this narrative is one we can easily recognise and relate to. This first family, and for every family since then, are quickly brought to the truth that the only hope and help they have in the struggles of life is found in the person of Jesus the Christ. While we concentrate on the family in these early verses, we will discover the story of Jesus weaving through the narrative. He is sometimes in the background, sometimes more apparent, but the verses are all there to begin to reveal the wonder of Jesus.

When God starts with the family, He begins with a man. To that man He then adds a woman. As we read the details we find ourselves wondering what we can reasonably expect in a relationship. When somebody comes into our lives, what can we reasonably expect out of that relationship? Even more than that, what can we expect when God brings someone into our life?

All of us are in families, all of us have relationships with different people. Should we expect to find perfection in any of those relationships? Why do we look for perfection in any relationship? Is there anywhere we can expect to find the perfect relationship?

> *then the Lord God formed the man of dust from the ground and breathed into his nostrils the breath of life, and the man became a living creature.* *Genesis 2:7*

Genesis one told us, God created man in the image and likeness of God. Here is chapter 2 we are told how He did that. He began by 'forming' man. The word 'form' is not the same word as the word 'create'. When God created, the word means He took nothing and brought something out of. This word 'formed' says God took something and made something out of it.

When God formed man, He took something that he could use to make something else, something different from it. He is a God who can create from nothing, but He is also a God who can take something in His hands and make something completely new out of it, something almost unrecognisable at first glance, and yet the original elements are still in evidence on closer inspection.

This word 'formed' speaks of taking something in hand and moving it around, of moulding it. When God made man, He took some dust in His hands and began to mould and shape something. Dust is not something which you can easily shape, but this Hebrew word translated 'dust' is a word which also speaks about soil.

Now there is a revelation here. Mankind was made out of two main elements. We were made out of soil, out of dirt, out of earth. It can still be very difficult to mold soil where there has been no rain for any length of time. At first sight that could be a problem, for how could dirt be moulded into shape? You can really only work easily with well moistened dirt.

In verse five and six we are told that the earth was watered by a mist that came up out of the ground. Some translations talk about streams coming up out of the ground, but the Hebrew word is not the word for stream. It is the word 'mist'. It speaks of a thick mist, or fog.

> *for the Lord God had not caused it to rain on the land, and there was no man to work the ground, and a mist was going up from the land and was watering the whole face of the ground.*
>
> *Genesis 2:5-6*

There are two ways that mist or fog is found. There is a mist which comes down from a moisture laden atmosphere. There is also a mist which comes up out of the land. This word for mist in Genesis 2 speaks of that mist which rises from the ground. When heat hits the soil, or rather gets to the water in the soil, it can produce a mist. At the beginning of this period rain does not fall from the sky. Actually there is no account of rain falling until the days of Noah in chapter six.

Maybe that was why the people of Noah's day never believed water would come from the sky and flood the earth. We find a similar incredulity from people when we read that God says He will finally remove the current earth with fire from the heavens. Too many think that can never happen and that the world will always carry on the way it is now, and even think it has never changed from it's present condition.

The earth was originally mingled with a good amount of water. If you take earth and then mix it with water you finish up with a kind of mouldable clay or mud. Mankind was moulded from dust and water. We are something like 90% water, the rest is this 'dust' material.

God took the dust, mingled with a large amount of water and began to mould mankind. In other words these verses picture God playing in the mud. He comes to play in the mud in order to make man out of the mud. A kind of mud man.

The revelation is we are made from dirt and water, mingled into mud. We are mud. We are little better than mud. So it is that the Psalmist says we are made out of the mud.

> *For he knows our frame; he remembers that we*
> *are dust.*   *Psalm 103:14*

Some of us are big mud, some are smaller mud, some are pretty mud, some ugly mud, but we are all mud.

We need to understand and remember, in any relationship which comes into our lives, we are dealing with mud, with dirt. God made us all out of mud, and when we are dealing with one another, we are dealing with mud. Some of the problems we have relating to one another are because we forget that we are only really dealing with mud.

Mud is what we are until the mud finally goes back into the ground. It is why God is going to come and say to man that He knows and understands us, we came from mud and we will return to mud.

There is a further Biblical revelation here in this picture of God in the mud. The word translated 'form' or 'mould' comes from the same root as the word 'Potter'. God, from the very beginning describes His activity in regard to mankind as the Potter who molds our clay.

He makes mud man, declares Himself to be the potter who is shaping man into what He desires. All we are is just plain and simple mud, until God then does something truly remarkable. He takes the mud man and adds something extraordinary to give us a living spirit within. It says He breathes, His breath, into the nose of the man He has made and makes us into living beings. He takes the dirt creature He has moulded and adds something of Himself to the dirt. The adding of Himself makes humanity "beings'. This word 'beings' is a word which speaks of the soul, of the self I am, of my desires, passions, appetites and emotions, it is His living breath. It makes us immortal creatures with the recognition and reality of eternity in our hearts.

Having made man out of the dirt, God makes a statement, which we dare not rush past and is all too often overlooked. He says, "It is not good for man to be alone." Which is startling if you only stop to think about it. God is good, and all that He does is good. Every time God had made something He has declared it to be good, except here. Here God makes man and says there is something about this part of His creation which is not good, there is a problem within it, it has a flaw included, a limitation revealed.

Because God is good, it must be true here that this flaw at least, this imperfection in what God did, has to have been done for a reason. God must have moulded and formed man like this deliberately. He must have set this flaw in place for His wise purposes to be fulfilled. It would be quite wrong, to suggest God made a mistake here. He has put this imperfection into the creation of man for a reason.

Not only does God say it is not good for the man to be alone, He then adds His intention to make a helper for man in order to overcome the limitation and flaw of the man being alone.

In chapter two we are then reminded that God has made all the other creatures, but none of them are to be the helper that a man needs. They are all named by the man, they are all to be governed and cared for by the man, but they are not the helper that man needs, nor are they the helper that God had always intended to make for man.

God looked at man and caused him to go into a deep sleep. While the man slept, God opened the side of this mud man and took out part of the mud that was there and made mud woman. As Adam slept God was still working. It is a reminder here in the beginning that this God neither slumbers nor sleeps, but that when we sleep, when we slumber, He is still working His purpose out for His creation.

He took part of the dirt from the man and made woman out of the same mud and in the likeness of the mud man. When the man woke from the sleep God presented the mud woman to the mud man who now turned and said, "this is now bone of my bones and flesh of my flesh." When the man said that it is recorded as Hebrew poetry. This man of dirt, wrote a poem. You can almost hear him singing. He sees the women and becomes poetic. He takes one look and bursts into verse.

I kind of wonder which way she was facing. Which part did he see that made him feel poetic? Whatever he saw, it made him lyrical, but even though he wrote a poem, the man is recorded only as speaking about the woman. We are not told whether he spoke to the woman about what he saw and felt, just that he spoke about what he saw. Now I know he might have spoken and told her what he thought, but we are never told that. The only thing you are told in the scripture is that when God brings mud women before him, he speaks to God. Let me put it like this, even at the very beginning the man seems to be more comfortable talking about the woman, than he is talking to the woman about how he felt.

All too often in a relationship, not only do we forget that we are dealing with mud, but there is also a problem in communication. Man often fails to deal well with his emotions, especially when it comes to him expressing them to the person he is emotional about.

As far as we can tell, in the whole of the scripture, in all the conversation, the man never tells the woman how he feels or discusses how beautiful he finds her. There was a problem in communication. The problem of communication between men and women is a vast one, for all too often men and women think differently and speak differently about the same things.

God made man and woman and He made us with this imperfection. Six times God in the creation narrative looked at something and said, that's good. That's good. That's good. That's good. That's very good. Only once, and that when he formed man did God look at what he made and say it was not good. Some want to translate this word 'good' here, with the word 'convenient'. But that creates a problem in the rest of the account because the Hebrew word used here is the same as that which is used over and over in those earlier verses. The biblical rules of interpretation would then mean that every time it should be translated by the word 'convenient'. God made the heavens and the earth and He put the sun in place, He said, well, that's convenient. That would seem to be a very strange assessment of His work.

When God made man, and looked and declared, 'that is not good', He is setting something up for us to understand. He is setting up a revelation for us to grasp that He made man with a flaw and He made woman from the flawed man.

When God declared it not to be good for a man to be alone at the very least, it tells us we were never meant to be isolated. God put a flaw within us, which means when we are on our own, we are likely to have a problem. It is never good to be alone and God's solution for this limitation He put within us, was to take this first husband, bring to him the first wife and get them to start a relationship and make a family.

When God said, it was not good for a man to be alone. He added these words "I will make him a helper fit for him".

The word helper does not mean cook or cleaner. It does not even mean housemate. Nor does the word have any connotation of inferiority within it. This word 'helper' is a deeply theological word which runs its way, right through the scriptures. It speaks of giving support, encouragement, strength, protection, nourishment, and care.

God looked at man and said he needs somebody to support him. He needs somebody to strengthen him. He needs someone to encourage him. He needs somebody to lift him up. He needs somebody to nourish him. That is what he needs as a man and then He made woman in the same image.

God then added to explain this helper was to be fit for the man. The Hebrew word translated 'fit' means 'before their eyes'. When we are eye to eye with somebody we are facing in opposite directions. This word 'fit' suggests there is something significantly opposite in what God was going to make which would encourage strengthen, nourish, protect, and care for the man, and something in the man that will, in turn, nourish, strengthen care for, encourage and protect the woman.

There is one more thing to notice about this couple made from mud. When mud dries out it becomes brittle. It becomes cracked. It becomes broken. Dirt needs a constant supply of water to keep it as mouldable adjustable mud.

The Lord Jesus talking one day to a lady as they were sitting by a well, said, if you drink of me, I will give you water which will rise up inside, that will give you life. All too often we finish cracked, broken damaged and Jesus says I can fix that because I can put the water back inside of you to refresh you, to mould you and to give you life.

We were never meant to be on our own, and the more we bring the water of God's spirit, the word of the living God, the health of God's strength, into every relationship, the sweeter life will be, the better our relationships will develop and the more we will be blessed as we live life in the family.

Beginnings

A garden paradise?

*"And the LORD God formed man of the dust of
the ground and breathed into his nostrils the
breath of life and man became a living soul."*
Genesis 2;7

The word Lord is in capitals as a reminder that the Hebrew
here uses the name God shared with Moses, at the burning
bush; the name Yahweh, or Jehovah. This God is the one who
is all we need Him to be, the ever present, all sufficient, all
knowing God. That God formed the man from the dirt. He
moulded the clay He moulded the mud together like a
Master Potter and shaped man.

He made us of dirt and then having moulded the dirt, He
breathed into the nostrils of man. God breathed into man
and when He breathed He did something really incredible.
He breathed into man the breath of life. The word translated
'breath' and the word 'life' are significant. 'Breath' is the same
Hebrew word as the word 'spirit'. So he breathed into man a
spirit of life.

God wants us to know that we may be made of mud but we
are more than just mud. God took the mud that was man,
and added some of His breath to you and to me, He added
part of Himself into us. He changed the whole nature of the
mud by putting some of Himself inside of us. In that
moment, man became a living soul. It says from that moment
on, there was something about God which had invaded
humanity. We are immortal souls. That means there is a life
within us that will not end. It is that part of us which never
seems to grow older. We feel the same, except we realise our
body, the mud bit, cannot do what once it was able to do. Or

if we do still manage to do it, it takes longer to recover than it used to take. Inside, we do not feel any older. Only when we look in the mirror we realise something about our mud has changed.

God comes and says, He made us what we are. He gave us life, and wants us to understand that the life He gave us is a life which is part of Him. That immortal soul is part of what He is, and we only truly live life in relationship with Him, because part of Him is within us. Now, I know that part is marred and damaged, but He comes and declares that He made us that we might know life and that our life should be complete only when He is within it.

Man became a living soul. Only to the extent that we live within the boundaries of God, will we ever fully know life and what it means to be truly alive.

The Lord God planted a garden eastward in Eden. And there He put the man in the garden whom He had formed.

> *And the Lord God planted a garden in Eden, in the east, and there he put the man whom he had formed. And out of the ground the Lord God made to spring up every tree that is pleasant to the sight and good for food. The tree of life was in the midst of the garden, and the tree of the knowledge of good and evil.*

As you read that it looks as though the Lord God made man and then planted the garden. But actually, the way it's put in the Hebrew is, having made man He then took the man into the garden which He had already planted.

It is like that in the Hebrew, because God wants us to realise that before ever the man was made, He had already provided for him. He does not wait till the man comes along and then think about making the provision for him. He is the God who sees a need beforehand and already sets the provision in place. He sees before. He visions 'pro' (before). He is the God of pro-vision.

In the account of the creation of this garden, every one of the Hebrew words used is important and powerful. The word 'garden' is significant because God uses a word which speaks of an area enclosed by a boundary.

God wants us to know when He made man He did not just leave him out in the universe, He did not even send man out into the earth. God made man and he said "I'm going to limit the area of your existence by a boundary". The boundary is set by a river, which splits into four streams which together set in place the extent of this garden.

God planted a set of boundaries, and the boundaries were in a place called Eden. This name 'Eden' occurs several times in Scripture. Nearly always it is talking about a different place. Nobody knows where this 'Eden' was, because the word Eden does not refer to a geographic location. The name Eden speaks of a 'place of delight', or a 'place of enjoyment'.

What we are told is that God set some boundaries in place, and within those boundaries, there is pleasure, enjoyment, and delight to be experienced. God then took the man and the woman He made to enjoy life with Him and put them within those boundaries, in a place of enjoyment, delight and pleasure. God wants to bless life with enjoyment and pleasure and He chooses to do that to the extent by which we live within His boundaries.

Verse nine explains that part of the delight and pleasure of the garden is the sheer variety and beauty of the trees God has planted in the garden. He has put every tree which is good to look at, and good for food there within this place of delight. In the midst of all these wonderful trees with all their variety, beauty and uniqueness, God planted two special trees. The tree of life and the tree of the knowledge of good and evil.

God really said "I am going to set in this garden, enjoyment, delight and pleasure. I am going to set every tree that is good to look at and every tree which has within them things that are good to eat." He has filled the area within the boundaries of this garden with trees, and those trees contain everything needed to look at nice things and to eat good things. Can you imagine what it must have been like? There would have been trees bearing apples, pears, plums, cherries, peaches, every kind of fruit tree, and every type of nut tree. We are intended to see God put every variety of tree in this garden for the delight and enjoyment of man. Then in the middle, He placed just two different trees. He put the tree of life and the Tree of the Knowledge of Good and Evil there.

The LORD God took man and put him in the garden. God told the man He had provided all that was needed for delight, enjoyment and pleasure in this garden, and then adds an amazing truth. The God who has made all this has a plan and a purpose for mankind. That plan and purpose was for man to 'dress' the garden and 'keep' the garden.

The word translated 'dress' means to live within and enjoy. The word translated 'keep' means to ensure the boundaries stay there. So God explains his task for mankind is for them to live within the boundaries of the garden, to maintain the boundaries He sets in place and to make sure those boundaries are kept fixed and secure, knowing that within those boundaries mankind can enjoy life to the full.

The picture of the relationship, plan and purpose God has for the man receives more insight from a further brief comment in this chapter of Genesis. God has showed Adam all the creatures He has made and asks Adam what they should call them. It is a brief aside, which speaks of a depth of relationship and pleasure.

Throughout the Bible the truth, that God has a plan and a purpose for each one of us, and sets boundaries for our life is constantly outlined. In Genesis 2 and at every other time the boundaries are laid out, God desires us to understand one truth. To the extent in which we live within the boundaries He sets down, and discover His plan for our lives and find purpose and fulfilment in His will and plan, we will walk in the blessing of the delight and enjoyment of a conscious awareness of His presence with us. His plan and purpose for each of our lives is that we might live within the boundaries of what He declares to be good for our enjoyment, our pleasure, our delight, and good for our relationship with God.

Remember what really turned the garden into a paradise, what gave the garden real significance, was not the variety of the trees, nor the beauty of the creation. What gave the garden value was not that the garden had been made by God, but rather the God who made the garden made it as a place for man to meet with Him. It is not so much the garden of God, as the God of the garden which determined this place as paradise. Anywhere without God is just another place, but any place where we meet God will become a paradise, a place of value and significance.

The Lord God gave commandment to the man with regard to what could be eaten. He said they could freely eat from any of the trees in the garden. The ESV translates this verse replacing the word freely with the word surely, then uses the word surely in the following verse where it says 'you will surely die'. But the Hebrew has two different and distinct words. Certainly speaking of the result of eating it is correct to translate the word 'surely die' but speaking of the ability to eat, there is no sense of the word surely, it is the idea of eating and eating to the full, which is why the King James version says you may freely eat.

We should not rush past this word 'freely'. God did not just say they could eat from every tree. He said the man could eat freely, or eat and eat and eat. God told him he could walk around within the boundaries He set, and can choose to eat whatever variety suited him and eat whenever he wanted.

In a world filled with the variety God made, there is the allowance of having preference, within the set boundaries. There are things which one person may choose whilst another person's preference may be different. God sets in place absolute and defined boundaries, and then within those limits He has placed preferential boundaries. There are things which will be one person's choice, which may not suit others, but as long as the preference choice, still maintains the established boundaries God sets there is freedom to choose.

God made man with the ability to choose what he wanted to do and what he wanted to eat. Man had the freedom and ability to choose, but within that freedom, God's desire is that for our choices to remain within the limits He reveals.

God says any variety, you can choose, as long as within that variety you stay within the boundaries set. It is true in every area of life. We may choose what to do and when to do it, and choose freely, but should also ensure that we know what God's boundaries are and live within them.

It is at this stage, having set the boundaries of the garden and establishing the ability of man to have and use freedom of choice that God puts in place a boundary as a prohibition. This is to be a fixed unchangeable boundary, with a warning upon it. It sets in place the reality that whilst we have freedom of choice, it is freedom within the limits that God sets.

We need to know, and recognise, the difference between established and immoveable boundaries and boundaries of preference and choice. Preference ones can be adjusted, others cannot be moved without there being the chance of us experiencing damaging consequences. Set your boundaries, let them be the boundaries that God set and then walk into life, knowing that within the boundaries, God wants to bless us. God wants us to enjoy life. But He says we can only truly enjoy life when we recognise the difference between allowable preference choices and the fixed unchangeable boundaries He has established.

Some people strike up a friendship and then a year down the line, they are trying to set some boundaries in place, it is a nightmare. They wonder why they are struggling in their relationship? The reason is, they never set the boundaries in place first. They walked into a friendship and then a while later on they have tried to set boundaries. It does not work, because one of them has a boundary somewhere and the other has set their boundary elsewhere. It leads to constant friction, because they are both working towards different aims with different limits.

The joy of the boundaries God sets in life is that we are free to choose. The problem of the boundaries that God sets is just this, we are free to choose. When God made us, He gave us the ability to freely choose. Here in the garden He now declares a prohibition. There is one tree, and only one tree from which they could not eat. God takes Adam and says 'see this tree in the middle of the garden, it is the tree of the knowledge of good and evil. See this tree do not eat from it. Every other tree you can eat freely from, but if you eat the fruit from this tree, on that day, you will surely die',

Here is the boundary. God prohibits one thing, within the boundary of all other preference and free choice. Only one fruit is excluded. That one thing has a punitive effect. In the centre of the garden there are two trees. The first tree was the tree of life. The second was the tree of the knowledge of good and evil. God said you can eat from any of the other trees within this garden except this one tree of the Knowledge of Good and Evil.

Bear in mind as we read this, that Eve has not been made at this stage. There is only God and Adam. The entire conversation takes place before Eve comes along. God is showing Adam the garden, He is giving Adam instruction about the relationship Adam has with God, and about the way that Adam is to live. By the time the woman comes along Adam already has a history. He has a purpose, an understanding and has been given instructions on the way he is to live.

When the woman comes along, she comes into a relationship which someone who already has a history and an understanding of what they are about. It is a reminder that every relationship we commence comes with both parties having a history and an understanding of life.

God gives this instruction to Adam. He warns him of the need to avoid the tree of the 'knowledge of good and evil'. From the day, God put Adam in the garden, mankind has been consumed with the pursuit of both those two trees in the centre of the garden, the tree of life and the tree of the knowledge of good and evil. Partaking of the tree of the knowledge of good and evil will change the whole relationship man has with God and affect the whole creation. Since that first prohibition from God mankind has given his time and effort struggling to hold on to life and pursuing knowledge.

God said there is just this one tree, you can freely eat from any of the others but not from this one tree. God is speaking to Adam, whose job was to look after the boundaries, to maintain the boundaries, for then there would be blessing in his life. Before God puts anybody else into his life, He set the boundaries, and explains that this is a punitive boundary. God told Adam, "You can freely choose any other, but that one tree will kill you." The phrase God uses is emphatic. It actually reads something like this, "you shall not ever eat from that one tree, because if you do you will not just die, you will surely and certainly die."

This tree which will kill Adam is in the middle of the garden. Imagine how many trees Adam had to pass just to get to that one tree. Only one tree is refused to him. In all the variety, only one will kill him. He has to pass by every other tree. He must refuse the food from all the other ones, just to get to that one tree, knowing that God says it will kill him. Imagine walking past all the trees that would have blessed him, but choosing to walk past them all, leaving his blessing behind him, just to reach the one which will kill him.

Have you ever thought about how much effort goes into sin? Look at everything you have to pass by, and all you have to go to, just in order to get to the one thing that will kill you. The catch is, the devil makes it look alluring and seem exciting, but God has told you it will kill you. It is not a chance, it is not a gamble, it is not even a multiple choice, it is an absolute certainty. It will kill you. The God who cannot lie has said so.

When we choose to pass by the blessings of God and choose to cross the boundaries, to transgress, we will die. We minimise sin, but God says we must not do it. But just like Adam, we see something which has caught our attention, our interest, our passion, but it is the one thing that God says, "It will kill you." We choose to transgress. It is not accidental, and God made it clear, when we sin, we die.

Remember Eve is not there. She will get the blame in a few verses, but she was not even there when God spoke this prohibition! Adam was supposed to tell her. He was supposed to explain to Eve that they must live within the boundaries that God set down. Adam was intended to explain that within these boundaries they were free to choose anything, to choose what suited them.

Somehow, the mud they were made from, the history he came with, the problems of communication they discovered, and one new character who enters their story leads them to be in a garden paradise and still choose the one thing that was prohibited. Then they wonder when they eat it why they had a problem that will kill them, damage their relationship with God and spoil the whole world.

Genesis chapter 2 finishes with this amazing revelation that neither the man or the woman knew shame. They were not dried out, they were not anxious about anything, they were not confounded or disappointed. They knew neither dejection or shame. All they knew was the joy and blessing of living in the abundance and variety of God's favour and presence.

What is deception?

In the first verse of the third chapter of Genesis, we are suddenly introduced to a new character. So far in this book of beginnings we have discovered something of the creation of the world and of everything within it. We have seen the creation of man and woman, and the way that God has placed them in a garden of delight and plenty. Then, all of a sudden, this third chapter, opens with this introduction of a completely new character.

We are left wondering where did he come from. In the Hebrew there is just one word, which is translated 'Now the serpent'. There is nothing said about his origin here. All we suddenly discover is that this new character is in the garden, in the midst of this paradise.

Too easily we think of everything in this garden being good. Some even believe God's ultimate plan is to get everything back to the way it was in Genesis 2. That would still leave a problem for us, an enemy roaming around. It was there, in that paradise that this one, described as 'the serpent', was moving around. At the very start of this third chapter there he is.

Everything seemed to be going so well. Everything God had made, as it is revealed to us in the first two chapters, is described either as good, or very good, with the sole exception being the issue of a man being on his own. Then suddenly we are introduced to this new character. Everything seemed to be alright, but with the arrival of the serpent we are led to wonder what is going on, because all it says is 'now the serpent.'

The first six verses in this third chapter contain a dialogue between the serpent and the woman. Previously there has been a dialogue between the man and God. But now in these first six verses neither the man or the living God are involved in the discussion. The dialogue is simply between the woman and the serpent.

If we read this passage, and think of this dialogue, just in terms of gender, we will miss what God has to say, we will fail to understand the revelation that God gives us here of life. In reality, this dialogue takes place between the serpent, and that part in all of us which is susceptible to his attacks. Every one of us is susceptible somewhere. I know some want to see this portion only in relation to the problems of 'women' but the truth is, any and all of us too easily fall under this kind of attack. It is not about gender, it is about all of us.

This new character is just introduced as the 'serpent' or the 'snake' and the word used can be translated by either term, but nowhere in the chapter does it tell us who the serpent is. It is just a dialogue between a serpent and a woman. A dialogue between a serpent and that part in all of us which is susceptible to the attacks of the evil one. Nowhere does it tell you who he is. He is just not identified, except by this word 'serpent'. In fact, if you read the whole book of Genesis, no where is the serpent identified as anything other than 'the serpent', or 'the snake'. Actually, if you read the whole of the Bible, you would read through the Old Testament on into the New Testament and only when you reach the twelfth chapter of Revelation is the serpent ever identified. In the ninth verse of that chapter, is the very first time he is identified.

> *that ancient serpent, who is called the devil and*
> *Satan, the deceiver of the whole world Rev. 12:9*

That is the first time he is identified. There are clues before. There are clues in the book of Job, in the book of Isaiah, and in the book of Ezekiel. But nowhere is the snake identified as Satan, until Revelation 12. Then in case you missed seeing that as you read the book, we find in Revelation 20:2 the serpent is once more identified as the devil, Satan.

We should understand this one truth, from this lack of being identified until the end of the whole story of the Bible, the devil does not normally come along and start any dialogue by introducing himself, and telling you who he is and explaining why he has come. Invariably his identity is hidden. We do not normally realise his identity, until after we have done something and find ourselves in a mess. He comes, and he tries to deceive us and trick us, but he never tells you who he is. He will often come under some disguise.

In this chapter in Genesis, it is very difficult to know, was the serpent actually Satan, or was Satan in the serpent, or even was Satan just speaking through the serpent? Sometimes in life, we come across Satan. Sometimes we come across Satan just working through somebody, and sometimes it is just somebody talking and using the words of Satan. He does not identify himself. Nowhere does it say who he is. If he came along and told you who he was, you could see him and realise what was going on. He does not identify himself because he always wants to do the same thing and only when you turn to the book of Revelation do you have a description of who he is and what he does.

There are clues about him, littered throughout the scriptures. The first thing we need to understand about him is this. He was not always bad. We do not know when he became bad. We do know he was originally made good. Because all that there is and ever was, came from the creating power of the living God. Since God created him and all that God ever did was good, God must have created him good at the start.

The Bible suggests he was not only made good at the beginning, but he was the wisest of all the creatures that God made. That is a revelation we need to grasp. He is wiser than we are. He was the wisest of all the creatures God ever made. Then we understand he was also made beautiful at the first. In fact, the book of Isaiah introduces him and says he was the most beautiful thing that God ever made.

He was made good, he was made wise, and he was made beautiful. And when he comes to us, he will often tend to come with his beauty, and his wisdom, and will customise what he says and does in order to try and trick us based on what we find attractive. When it comes to disobeying God, what you find attractive may not be what I find attractive. What I find attractive, just in life may not be what you find attractive. But the enemy will come and he will customise his deception to fit what each of us finds attractive.

He started good. God made him good. But God gave him the ability to choose. Just as God gave you that ability. Satan chose to set himself up against God. He chose to come against God and declare himself to be at least as good as God.

In that moment, his goodness became bad. And from that moment on, he began to use his wisdom, attractiveness and cunning to seek to harm and damage anything that God does. He longs to pull us away from God and ruin all that God wants to do for our good.

I go to the doctors once every few years normally. One of the things they tend to always ask as they go through a list of health checks is whether I smoke. I always say 'no'. Then they look and ask if I have ever smoked. Again I say 'no'. One day one of the medics asked me why I had never smoked. I told him it had just never appealed to me. Some of my school friends had smoked and had tried to get me to try it. But I looked and in truth it just never seemed pleasant or attractive to me. Now, I am not saying smoking is evil. That is not my point here. I just use this simple illustration to suggest that in life there are things that appeal to some and not to others.

The devil will customises his approach to each of us, based on the things that attract each of us. He comes with an understanding of who he is dealing with. He knows what suits us. He knows what attracts us. He knows what appeals to us. He customises the way he comes, based on how we are, not how the person next to us is. But, before we look any further at these verses in Genesis, know this, the devil is understandable, and he is beatable.

Revelation 12:9, tells us exactly what his ploy is, what he comes to do. It says, he comes to deceive the world. That word 'deceive' is a little Greek word which means 'to lead astray'. It means 'to take out of a place of safety'. It means 'to encourage to cross a boundary'. It means 'to entice you to go further'. He wants to take us further than we would go, if we just took the time to pause and think about what we were doing.

He always comes with the same thing. He comes with the aim of taking us away from God, to lead us away from God, to cause us to move from the safety and security of our relationship with God and with God's people. His desire is to lead us into a place where he can entice us to do something that will break our fellowship with God and our fellowship with God's people. He always does the same thing. His only aim is to keep us away from God. In these six verses at the start of Genesis three, we can discover how he does it.

"Now the serpent was more subtle," he was more crafty, he was more deceitful than any other creature. The serpent came to the woman and she did not realise he was a trickster. He hid what he wanted to do. Because all he wants to do is take her away from God.

The first thing he did when he turned up was to say something to the woman. So often his deceit will start with a conversation. He starts with a conversation, he starts with a desire to have a discussion. The whole aim of the discussion is to take her away from God. That is his hidden aim, but he starts with a discussion and he starts the discussion with something that is going to get her interest.

The second thing to notice is the content of this conversation. The serpent suggests they should have a chat about God. Here is the devil, and he starts by saying to the woman, "let's talk about you and God". Notice he is using words, he is going to quote God, but his aim, his purpose is to lead her away from a place of safety in order to damage her relationship with God.

He comes and says, "Let's have a chat. Let's talk about you and God. Let's see how you are doing." And then he says, "What did God say to you? tell me about the conversation you have had with God. Did God actually say neither of you could eat anything in the garden?" The woman responds by saying, "We may eat of the fruit of the trees of the garden, but of the fruit of the tree, which is in the middle of the garden, God said, 'you shall not eat of it, neither shall you touch it, lest you die'."

Now the woman had not actually heard what God said, she only knew what the man told her God said. God actually said "the day you eat it, you will surely die". He never said they could not touch it, although that may have been good advice, based on the prohibition of eating from it. The other thing God told them was that the day they ate it, they would surely, definitely die. The woman's report was that they 'might die', or 'in case we die'. Her words record a minimising of the consequence of going against the word of the living God.

Once the enemy has us in a conversation, the debate he will always try to engage us with, has to do with what God actually said. He knows exactly what God has said, and can quote it if he chooses to, but if he can get us to misquote it, he is on the way to causing us to doubt the veracity and minimise the fullness of all that God declares. He does this in a way that is subtle.

Having the woman tell him what God had said, and knowing she has not fully and accurately repeated what God said to the man, the enemy now comes with his next step. He moves from his first statement "Did God really say that." to bring further uncertainty into the woman's mind with a statement which now aims to casting doubt on to the very nature of the God who cannot lie. He suggests she will not really die, but instead if she only ate, she would know so much more, her eyes would see and understand what is good and what is evil. She would be able to see fully and properly, what at the moment she does not see or understand, she would become like God. It is his next ploy. "If you do this, you will understand so much better, and you will be just like God."

With that we are told the woman looked at the tree. She gazed at the tree. The enemy now attacks her emotionally and intellectually. She looks at the tree and sees it looks good for food, it is pleasing to the eye and she is told the result of eating will be good, it will increase knowledge.

The enemy comes to attack her based on her physical needs with something that looks good. We all have needs, our bodies have needs and the God who made us, chose to create us with those needs. The woman looked at the tree. Not only did it look as though it would satisfy her needs, it seemed to be so pleasant to the eye. The word translated 'pleasant' is a word which speaks about something being 'desirable'. It talks about attractiveness.

The enemy also attacks theologically. He says you do not need to worry about this. He says 'God knows that on the day she chooses to eat from the forbidden fruit she will be just like God.' He is asking the woman to doubt the truthfulness of God to question whether God really is good and wonder if He is really concerned to ensure we have the best for us. He throws uncertainty over whether God really has put in place all that we need for life and for godliness.

The enemy attacks her theologically, his complete argument suggests that God is just on an ego trip. He says God is worried that humans might be as great and as good as God. It is not possible. We will never be close to becoming the same as the eternal, almighty, omnipresent, omniscient holy God. Never loose sight of the truth that God will never forget us, and only ever thinks and plans for ways to bless, to prosper, to favour and lead us into life.

She looks at the fruit on the tree knowing that God said it is not good for you, but the serpent suggests to her that it looks good, and it did look good, didn't it? He attacks on an emotional and intellectual front asking her to think about her physicality. He knows that if we give in to those needs, against the word of God, he has won and we have been deceived. Because deception always makes right look wrong, and wrong look, right.

Then he attacks her spiritually. In these verses in chapter 3, both the woman and the serpent address God, just as God. Up until this point God has always been referred as the "Lord God". But the enemy moves the conversation by refering to him just as God. This God is the Lord God. He is Lord of creation and Lord in covenant. Now he is spoken of just as God, just as a higher power, because if the enemy can get her to forget that this God is Lord of all, the enemy has won. God is not so much just God as He is the Sovereign Lord.

So the enemy comes and by his subtle shift in the name of God suggests forgetting about this Lord thing. He invites her to chat about God. The devil does not mind us being spiritual. The devil does not even mind us believing in God. He believes in God. His desire is not to move us from believing in God, but to move us from making and keeping the living God as the Lord of our life.

There is a day when every knee will bow and every tongue will confess that Jesus Christ is Lord to the glory of God the Father. To all of us, the enemy comes, and is happy for us to believe in God. We can talk about God, we can talk about religion, we can talk about spirituality. The problem for the enemy is when we agree with the Scripture and make Jesus the Christ, Lord of our lives. This Jesus must be the Lord our God. He is the master of our life. He made us for Himself.

He redeemed us for Himself. He alone has the right to be Lord over all that we are, all that we have, and all that we do.

The aim of the enemy is to take us from God, he will get us to doubt God's Word. He will introduce conversations and thoughts and plans about God which are not true, are not honest, and are not centred on Jesus, the Christ. He will attack our physicality; he will attack us intellectually, theologically, and spiritually, aiming at our emotions and our intellect, aiming to deceive. He comes and suggests what is right is really wrong, and what is wrong is actually right. Then when we are deceived he takes us away from God, leaving us in a mess, existing with the consequences of the deception we have fallen under.

Despite all that, this subtle, craft clever enemy can be beaten.
> *that ancient serpent, who is called the devil and Satan, the deceiver of the whole world—he was thrown down to the earth, and his angels were thrown down with him. And I heard a loud voice in heaven, saying, "Now the salvation and the power and the kingdom of our God and the authority of his Christ have come, for the accuser of our brothers has been thrown down, who accuses them day and night before our God. And they have conquered him by the blood of the Lamb and by the word of their testimony, for they loved not their lives even unto death. Revelation 12:9-12*

It says when it comes to the old serpent there are three ways to overcome him. You need all three.

The first element to be able to overcame the serpent is a recognition and dependence on the blood of the Lamb. I do not know if you have ever heard anyone talking about pleading the blood. The enemy will not be over concerned if we go to church or become religious. As long as we never reach the point where we realise the value and voice of the blood of Jesus. The blood that Jesus shed has the power to break the power of the enemy. That blood which Jesus shed for us way back on Calvary. Even though it was years ago, that blood will never lose its power.

> *The blood that Jesus shed for me*
> *Way back on Calvary*
> *The blood that gives me strength from day to day*
> *It will never lose its power.*

> *It soothes my doubts and calms my fears*
> *And it dries all my tears,*
> *The blood that gives me strength from day to day*
> *It will never lose its power.*

> *It reaches to the highest mountain*
> *It flows to the lowest valley*
> *The blood that gives me strength from day to day*
> *It will never lose its power*
> ©*Andrae Crouch*

His blood washes us from sin. His blood overcomes the curse the enemy wanted to keep us under. His blood has the power to break every sin, every curse, every sickness, every disease, every weapon that comes against us.

Then these verses in Revelation tell us that the enemy was overcome by the word of their testimony. There are at least two ways to understand this.

First you could read the phrase with a capital 'W'. The word with a capital W talks of Jesus the Christ. They overcame him by their testimony to the Word of God. It was not just by the blood, but by their relationship with Jesus the Christ. They overcame him because they walked with Jesus Christ. They overcame him because they talked with Jesus Christ. Every time that the enemy came and tried to trick them. They went back to the Word, they went back to the Saviour, they looked again to examine the Word, they sought to find Jesus, they begged on their knees, that God might touch them through the power of the risen Christ, and He gave them His power to overcome everything.

Then you can read the 'word of their testimony' with a little 'w'. They overcame the enemy because they had a living testimony of all that Jesus was and meant to them. Their testimony was their story. They had a story to tell of all they had found in their relationship with the living God, made possible through their trust in Jesus the Christ. Even in the middle of storms, their testimony was certain. However dark it seemed, they knew God who was able to carry them through as overcomers.

Then the third element we need to overcome the enemy is the recognition that whatever he throws at us, what ever he entices us with, it is not to be compared with the wonder of knowing the living God as our Lord and Saviour. Revelation declares that even when they were about to be killed, they had settled this one thing, nothing would ever separate them from the love of God. They were determined to finish strong rather than be led astray. Death in this world, in any case, is, for those who know God for themselves, nothing but the entry into a sweetness of the paradise of His immediate presence.

Beware of the enemy, understand the plans and ploys of the enemy, realise his skill and craftiness, but recognise he can and is beaten by the blood of Jesus, the testimony of Jesus, our testimony in Jesus, and our recognition that whatever is offered to entice us with during our life here on the earth is not worth being deceived and looses far more than it ever gains or even offers.

The entry of sin

Genesis, chapter three started with the conversation between the serpent and the women. While the conversation is between the serpent and the woman the unfolding discussion is not about gender, it is a conversation between the serpent and that part of mankind which is vulnerable to his craft and lies. The enemy customises his approach and appeal to the different appetites that attract each of us. He comes and questions the authority of God and the Word of God.

Now the woman had not been created when the exclusion of eating from the one tree was given by God to the man, but she must have known something of what God said because the serpent came and talked about what God had declared and in reply she paraphrased some of what God said.

She was not there in the moment God set the boundary, but had she been told exactly what God had said? Did she understand the words that God said to the man. Had she grasped the extent of the consequences of eating from that one tree? If she had been there when God set the exclusion, would she still have eaten from the tree?

She must have heard something, in order to be able to paraphrase what God had said. But I wonder whether she had ever really heard the word of God.

The biblical concept of hearing involves two things. First of all it involves the revelation of God entering our ears, but it also involves an appropriate response to the revelation which has entered our ears. Those two things are always there. That is always true of hearing. We all know of those times in life when either we said or somebody has said to us, "did you hear what I said?" If someone says that to us we tend to try to go back in our minds in an attempt to replay the previous few moments, because what we are being told is that while the sound of the words may have entered our ears the expected response has not been forthcoming. We try to replay the moments, in order to respond, and in doing so we accept we were never truly listening in a way which meant we heard what was being said. The sounds entering our ears together with the making of an appropriate response are both necessary for it to be true to say we have heard what was said. The biblical concept of hearing is always the same. It requires a revelation to come to us and an appropriate response to that revelation being made by us.

Had the woman heard what God had said? If she had heard and understood what had been said by God, why did she still disobey? If she really understood the prohibition, and the declared consequences, why did she do it? If she knew that eating was disobedience, and was an action against the revealed word of God, why did she intentionally and deliberately cross the boundary? Why did she transgress? Why did she sin? Did she hear God's word, and if she did hear, what did she do with what she heard?

God had said, they may freely eat of all the trees except this one because if they ate from this one, in the same day they would surely die. The discussion with the serpent has taken place and then Genesis three verse 6 says "she took of the fruit and ate". She deliberately, consciously, intentionally used her will to go against what God said. Why would she do that? The real question we should ask at this point is, why would any of us do that?

We are the same. We know what God says. We know what

God prohibits. We know what God requires, and yet we deliberately, consciously, intentionally engage our will and choose to go against God. Why would we do that? Do we doubt God's word, would we question His character and desire for our best?

There are a number of possibilities of why we go against the declared word of the living God. Maybe we do not understand what God says. Maybe we think that is not really what God said. Perhaps we think that is not really what God meant. Maybe we realise it is wrong, but someone else is doing it and they seem to have got away with it. Possibly we know exactly what is said, but we think we will be able to handle the consequences. Did we hear what God said? Did we know and understand the boundaries He set for our life?

The truth is, we hear what God says and we all knowingly disobey, we all use the power of our own wills and deliberately fly in the face of what God said. The Bible reminds us:

all have sinned . . .   *Romans 3:23*
    and also
The soul who sins shall die.   *Ezekiel 18:20*

The woman took the fruit from the tree and ate it. She ate and now knew the difference between good and evil, she understood the concept of doing right and doing wrong, she knew it from experience. She now knows what death is really like. She knows what evil is and how it feels.

Despite all of that, we then read,
    she also gave some to her husband who was with
    her, and he ate.   *Genesis 3:6*

If she knew that what she had done was wrong, why would

she give the fruit to the man and get him to be a part of her deliberate and wilful disobedience? She knows it is wrong, she knows what the effect is, she knows going into this is sin, but she gave to the man so he could eat also. Why would anyone invite somebody else to join them in their sin? Why would you want a sin partner?

Some have suggested, she gave the man the fruit, because she loved him and wanted him to be a part of sharing her experience. The kind of suggestion that comes from "if you loved me, you would do this with me." Know that form or argument is always a lie. If they loved you, they would not ask you to share in any deliberate and open defiance of God's word.

Why did she do it? The simple answer is she was deceived. Sin is always a deception. The word deception means "to lead off the right way, to entice and seduce off the track". Deception looks at things and sees them in a different way to what they really are. Deception makes us look at right and think it looks wrong. It makes us see wrong and think it is right. It changes the way we see things, until instead of seeing what is really there, we see something completely different. The key to the falling into sin is always deception. The woman was deceived.

Remember, this is not about gender. The woman was deceived. When it says she ate and then gave some to Adam who must have been there, it is the first time in these six verses, we are made aware of his presence at the discussion. He must have been there. Yet he never said a word, he never made a comment. The woman was deceived, but this is not about gender, or about some fictional problem to do with women. The Apostle Paul comes to this story and writes:

> *Adam was not deceived, but the woman was deceived and became a transgressor.*
> *1 Timothy 2:14.*

Paul says Adam was not deceived. Eve was deceived and she became a transgressor. In reading those words to Timothy,I wonder how anybody has ever suggested that the entry of sin into the world was the woman's fault. Yet you can come across those who claim women got us into this mess, and from that build a whole false teaching about the role of gender. It was never about gender. Look at what the Scripture actually says and teaches, read the words that are actually given without any preconception. Paul speaking of the eating of the prohibited fruit declares that Adam was not deceived, but the woman was.

There are two words in Greek for being deceived. Both words speak of being led astray, being seduced to do something that is wrong, of being caused to wander aside. Both have the same idea and both have the same meaning. The first word for deception is the one which appears here speaking about Adam. It has a negative added so that it reads 'Adam was not deceived'. It means Adam was not led astray. The second word comes from the same root but it has something added at the beginning of it as a prefix. That prefix changes the meaning from a word which just speaks of being deceived into a word which speaks of being 'totally deceived', completely tricked and totally seduced into doing wrong.

Those two words show us that there are gradations, or levels of deception. One simply means to be deceived, whilst the other speaks of being completely and totally deceived.

In this verse in the epistle to Timothy we read that Adam

was not deceived. He was not even led astray but the woman was completely seduced, tricked and totally deceived.

That begs a question. She was totally deceived, Adam was not even deceived, but they both ate from the tree. She ate first, having been totally deceived, she became a transgressor. Then she gave to the man and he ate. He was not deceived or led astray. That has to mean that Adam chose to eat with his eyes wide open.

Which of them then, brought sin into the world? The Apostle Paul, who wrote this epistle to Timothy, also writes a letter to the church in Rome. Having said to Timothy, Adam was not deceived, but the woman was deceived, he writes to the Roman Christians and says, it was the man who brought sin into the world.

> *sin came into the world through one man, and*
> *death through sin, and so death spread to all men*
> *because all sinned*   *Romans 5:12*

Paul does not say the woman brought sin into this world. He is very clear that sin came into the world because of the action of the man. Sin entered because of what the first man did. The problem came with the first Adam and the solution to sin in the world comes by the actions of the second Adam.

At the start of Genesis three, the discussion is between the serpent and the woman, though we discover the man was there, he takes no part in the conversation. The serpent causes the woman to doubt the character and word of the living God. He deceived her to think that what God said was not true, and that what God said would happen, would not take place. The interaction is between the serpent and the woman. Now she is deceived. Verse 6, tells the next interaction. It is between the woman and the man. "She gave to him and he did eat."

When the serpent had not deceived Adam, why did he then eat. He saw her eat, and then when she gave some to him, he took it, and he ate also. Nobody made him, nobody forced him, he chose to eat after his wife had eaten. He was not totally deceived, but he still ate.

Why did Adam chose to eat? In that moment something mattered more than his relationship with God, and every death, every sorrow, every trouble, every destruction, every sin, every pain and every curse came into the world. All because he chose not to put God first.

Adam will choose to blame others for eating, but before he even took and ate, he knew it was wrong. She shared her sin with him, but he took without even being deceived. If the enemy can find somebody who is weak enough not to know God's authority and God's word, he is halfway there to winning.

If the serpent can put someone like that into our lives, he is on his way to taking control of both of us. When there is anything or anyone in our life that matters more than our relationship with the living God we find ourselves in a perilous position.

The Apostle Paul takes up the narrative from Genesis three as he writes to the church in Corinth. Corinth is a really interesting city. It was known for its impurity, its idolatry, its godlessness. It was known as a society which stood totally and completely against everything the living God declared and everything that God said should be done.

There in Corinth a young church had been founded. It was still a fragile young church. Every church is fragile. It is one of the easiest thing in the world to break. The enemy desires to break local churches, to bring division and destruction.

Paul is writing a further letter to this church in Corinth and is reminding them of his relationship with them. He says he is like a father with a daughter. A father who is desirous of coming to give the daughter away in marriage. He writes:

> *I feel a divine jealousy for you, since I betrothed you to one husband, to present you as a pure virgin to Christ. But I am afraid that as the serpent deceived Eve by his cunning, your thoughts will be led astray from a sincere and pure devotion to Christ. For if someone comes and proclaims another Jesus than the one we proclaimed, or if you receive a different spirit from the one you received, or if you accept a different gospel from the one you accepted, you put up with it readily enough.*
> *2 Corinthians 11:2-4*

He says I am jealous for you because I have promised you to a husband. He says he is waiting for the day when he will be able to walk this daughter to her marriage and on that day she will be pure and holy.

In Paul's day and culture, when a daughter was promised in mariage, she spent the next year living in her Father's house. Living there, she lived by his rules. The father's job was to make sure that all the time, until they came to the wedding, she would be kept pure and holy.

Paul writes to this fledgling church, knowing one day, he will have to give answer before the living God for these people.

He says, he fears, he is afraid for them. King James says "I fear, lest by any means", the word is "somehow" in the way the serpent tricked Eve and totally deceived her, your minds might be corrupted and your thoughts led astray from a sincere and pure devotion to Christ.

It does not talk about an untaught and ignorant faith. God help us. He says, he has tried to deliver to them the faith of purity and devotion to the living God to keep them together as the people of God, but the enemy has a desire to persuade them to move to some form of religion which is easier, cheaper, and cost them nothing.

The story in Genesis, shows what happened, the enemy came to take them away from God's authority, from doing things in God's way, and from following His Word in absolute perfection. See what the enemy did, he tricked her and moved her away from her devotion to the purity and authority of the Word of God. Paul says if anyone lets the enemy do that, they will be deceived, just like Eve and fall the same way she did.

Paul then talks of a further fear he has that somebody would come and bring in some spirit other than the holy spirit, who is the spirit of love and purity. Or that they should bring in some other gospel that is not good news at all and suddenly his readers may think their salvation and sanctification is all down to what they do, instead of realising it is all down to what God has done for them in Jesus the Christ. He says he worries that some new preacher will come and they will settle for less than the only way, the only truth and the only life that is found in Jesus. He worries because the enemy is out to destroy what God has done and they are deceived and accept something other than God.

Paul's concern rings so relevant to us today, when there are so many who claim to be followers and teachers of the living God, who then look to remove some bits from the Scripture, adjust other parts to suit their own thinking and the ways of the world, and all they are really engaged in is doing the work of the enemy of souls, that old serpent as they try to show that what God says is wrong, is actually alright, and what God says is good, is maybe not all that wonderful.

In our world, the good news is, Jesus is coming again, but he has not come yet. God the Holy Spirit is still able to move hearts and lives, speaking about those areas which are wrong and need to be changed. God speaks to us because He loves us and wants to draw us back into the right path that we might walk in the blessing of His free provision.

Our point of deliverance always starts at the point of deceit. The deceit started with the rejection of the authority of the Word of God. Our deliverance comes at the point of receiving and believing God's Word, reading what God says, accepting the truth of what God says, and trusting our lives to be and do all that God declares. Even for those who like me may have been deceived and fallen into sin and error, the living God comes and declares the moment we turn back to Him, He receives us, cleanses us, and makes us pure again.

The writer of the book of Proverbs puts it in this way
> *for the righteous falls seven times and rises again,*
> *but the wicked stumble in times of calamity.*
> *Proverbs 24:16*

Even righteous men fall. They fall seven times. They can fall over and over again. In spite of our devotion to purity and holiness, we can fall, many times. The issue is just this, when a righteous man falls, he does not stay fallen. He rises again. What matters most is not how many times we may fall over, it only matters that we get up one more time than we fall. We get back up, by the power of the life that lives within us, through the Holy Spirit, That same power which raised Jesus from the dead, causes the child of God who falls to rise back up again. The Bible says a righteous man gets up one more time than he falls, for every time he falls he turns back to the living God who can pick him back up.

Learn how easily we also can be fully deceived, just like Eve. Realise, we can also bring sin into our lives, even though we know it is wrong, just like Adam, but that through the wonderful substitutionary death and resurrection of Jesus the Christ we can know forgiveness, life and godliness, so that even if we fall, the power that works within us will cause us to rise back up again and keep on walking in fellowship with the living God, until the day when He welcomes us into the immediacy of His glorious presence and ensures we stand in eternity, complete, pure and holy.

Responses to sin

The woman, having been totally deceived by the serpent, took from the one thing God had prohibited, consumed that one thing and then gave the same prohibited fruit to the man who also took and ate. The moment they did this they discovered the truth of God's warning and their immediate response to crossing the line of God's truth begins to be unpacked next in this book of beginnings.

> *Then the eyes of both were opened, and they knew that they were naked. And they sewed fig leaves together and made themselves loincloths.*
>
> *Genesis 3:7*

In the moment they ate, their eyes were open. Once their eyes were open, they immediately realized they were naked. The word naked in the Hebrew comes from a word which means to be exposed.

The last verse in Genesis 2 told us they were both naked, but that their nakedness was without shame. They were exposed but had no understanding or experience of what is was to feel shame. But immediately they did wrong, they knew what it was to be exposed and to experience shame over what they had done. The first result of their action was to know shame. They are uncovered and ashamed.

Experiencing the shame which followed their disobedience, their immediate reaction was an attempt to cover themselves. It was the first thing they thought of. There appears to have been no attempt to talk about their sin, just an attempt to cover up the shame that followed exposure.

Their efforts to cover themselves from the shame they felt

following their disobedience appears not only to be an attempt to remove the awareness of shame but also includes an attempt to make the consequences of their sin not just acceptable but attractive. They went to a fig tree, they took some leaves from the tree and making a garment of leaves to cover their nakedness they sought to make themselves look beautiful. It was the first attempt at creative fashion.

It is interesting to notice that all they tried to cover up at this stage, was their loins. They made a belt, a loincloth to cover their nakedness. It may be that Paul had this in mind when he wrote in Ephesians that we are to have our loins covered with truth. Paul uses a word for truth, which speaks not merely of spoken truths, but of truth in terms of reality, of sincerity, of truth in the moral sphere, of straightforwardness and integrity.

They made a belt to cover their loins, to try to minimise the wrongdoing and cover up the consequences they felt.

As men and women, our first response to doing wrong often is still an attempt to cover up the result and to make the consequences appear better than the reality of our sin.

The next thing the pair experienced was an awareness of God, of the sound of God, or the voice of God as the Lord God came walking in the Garden.

> *And they heard the sound of the LORD God walking in the garden in the cool of the day, and the man and his wife hid themselves from the presence of the LORD God among the trees of the garden.* Genesis 3:8

As soon as they were aware of God coming near, they ran

and hid. The Lord God was walking in the garden in the cool of the day and realizing they were no longer perfect, knowing shame and aware of the change in the way things looked, they sought to run from Him, and began to try to hide from the very presence of God.

They tried to hide themselves from where God was present. They sought to hide from hearing what God had to say, and they ran away from being where they could commune and worship the living God.

There is something uncomfortable about being in an atmosphere of worship, when you are trying to cover up your sin. God was just doing what he always did. He was turning up to meet with them, and they sought to be where God would not see them or speak to them.

Now, we know you cannot ever be where God cannot see you, for while it is true that He is of purer eyes than to gaze on sin, He is also the God who is everywhere. It is impossible to be where He is not. You can never hide where He cannot see. The omnipresent, and all seeing God always knows everything about us and anywhere we are.

Even though God knows where they were, verse nine tells us that the Lord God called to Adam and said, "Where are you?" He looked and called out to Adam. The word "you" is in the masculine, singular. They both ate, they both heard the voice of God coming in the garden, they both hid, and God specifically called out to Adam. He is coming looking for Adam first. He is seeking out the transgressor.

Adam now replies to the question of God, "I heard the sound of you in the garden, and I was afraid, because I was naked, and I hid myself." The word translated 'sound' is a word which speaks of the sound of a voice. Adam explained he heard the voice of God, and he was afraid, he was ashamed, and so he ran and hid. Those three statements suggest the problem that men face. They are afraid, they are exposed, they hid themselves. He was afraid of meeting God. He has become afraid of the God who has only ever blessed him. Understand what sin does. Adam was afraid, he was exposed and ashamed, he ran and hid.

It is what sin does to Adam, and understand sin creates the same response and reaction in all of us. Everyone in the whole of humanity has found the same experience. First of all we feel exposed and experience shame. Then we try and run from God. We try and hide. Ultimately we are afraid of coming anywhere God might be found, and set out to find someone else to blame for what we have done, excusing ourselves from any responsibility for our actions.

Knowing all there is to know about what has taken place, God still chooses to speak to Adam. He asks Adam, whether he ate of the prohibited fruit. God is trying to get the man to confront what he has done and admit his wrong. All the way through this third chapter, from the minute God first turns up in verse seven, He is looking to speak to Adam, He is reaching out to him.

God calls and reaches out to Adam. He knows the best way to restore their broken relationship, is for the man to go back to the place where he wandered from God or chose to disregard Him and His word, and admit his fault.

Adam response is to claim nothing was his fault. Instead of him, he chooses to blame the woman. As he seeks to shift the blame he uses three different arguments, all of which are intended to absolve him from any guilt. I guarantee we have all tried these three excuses at some time or other as we attempt to shift the blame for our own faults. First of all he tries to say it was not down to him, it was somebody else. Then he uses the excuse of someone else making him do what he did. We all know the response which claims it was not my fault, it was someone else. But the choice is yours. We have a free choice to do wrong.

His next attempt to shift the blame is outrageous. He says it was all down to God, after all, it was God who had given him the woman. His claim is that if God had not done what He had done for Adam, Adam would never have done wrong. He blames the living God, who had never done anything but bless him.

Those are the three, so often heard excuses, "It was not me", "they made me do it", "It is really God's fault"!

Having spoken to the man, God turns to the woman and asks her what happened and she brings up another common excuse, as she also seeks to shift the blame. Her response has an almost spiritual ring to it. She claims, it was the serpent, all down to the subtlety of Satan. If it is not my fault, or my friend's fault, and it was not God's fault, then it must have been the devil.

That is a really popular excuse in some circles. It has fuelled a whole area of 'ministry' known as 'deliverance ministry.' Now I know there are times when the enemy of souls will enslave men and women, binding them with strong chains. But most of the time, we do wrong, because we choose to do wrong. We satisfy the appetite which we find attractive and the enemy has done little more than draw our attention to that desire. Most times it is not the devil who did it. I know he tricked us. But we chose all by ourselves to think and do that which is contrary to the will and word of God.

It is interesting to look through the whole Genesis three, and notice, once the serpent has deceived the woman, the man and woman having sinned, the serpent never says another thing in the story. When the devil has messed a life up, deceived someone and they have chosen to go against God, and His word, he just sits down watching to see what will happen next. His response is to say nothing more, he has achieved his purpose to mess up what God has done. But while he says nothing openly, understand, he is still there.

The serpent thinks he has won, he has got to the man and the woman. He has brought death and destruction, shame and fear upon them, and he thinks there is nothing else that he needs to do.

He has not changed, he still deceives. His aim is still to get people to go against God. His aim is to encourage us to run away from God. He will do anything to keep us from the presence of God and the worship of God. He will allow us to do anything, even good things, as long as he can keep us from ever hearing what God has to say. He desires to keep us in fear, to keep us running from God. He loves us to stay in a place where we refuse to own our sin. He desires us to always carry our guilt and shame. Because all he ever wanted to do was mess up and destroy the work of God and especially as it is seen in the real vital relationship we can have with this living, loving and holy, Lord God.

Whenever we read this third chapter of Genesis, the response of man and woman to sin is something we recognise. The serpents response to sin is unchanged, but the response of the living Lord God should always amaze us.

God called out to Adam and asked where he was. He is the God who sees and knows everything. This is the God who is everywhere. This God we can never hide from. He was not telling Adam, He did not know where he had got to. He already knew. He already knows where we all are at. Verse nine says God called out to Adam, to the man, and said "where are you." The implication is not just that God called out indiscriminately to any who would hear Him, but rather that He called out "Adam, where are you." He is speaking to Adam by name. It is a personal call to Adam. He is reminding Adam He knows his name, and really declares, "whatever the mess, I know who you are, and I still have something I want to say to you."

Notice the gentle grace of God. When Adam responds to say he heard God coming, was afraid, because of his nakedness and hid. Even though God knew all that has happened, He does not come accusingly to Adam, or to Eve. Instead He says to Adam, "what did you do, have you done what I said not to do." Instead of confronting and accusing Adam with his sin, He invites Adam to acknowledge his sin and confess to what he had done.

This is the God who already knew, what had been done. Nothing escapes His notice. But He knows that to reach you and me, and do for us what he chooses to do, He has to get us back to where we messed up.

Once God has spoken, and Adam has blamed the woman and then blamed God Himself, God never argues or accuses him. You might have expected God to object at either excuse. He might reasonably have objected at being blamed Himself, but God never goes there. Instead He turns to the woman and asks her what she has done. Now the woman follows the lead of her husband and blames somebody else. She says it was the serpents fault. The serpent deceived her and so she ate. Once more God says nothing more to the woman at that point. You might expect Him to have pointed out her folly, but instead God turns to the serpent.

God turns to the serpent, He never asks anything of that crafty creature. This time, and for the first time God pronounces a curse. God never cursed Adam, He never even cursed the woman. God started with that old serpent, and He says "You are cursed, forever, and for all of time, I will put enmity between you and your children, and the woman and her offspring."

We need to understand that from that moment on there are going to be two races, two distinct groups, one that will be described as the children of the serpent, and the other who will be known as the children of the seed that will come from the woman. There will always be enmity between these two.

Have you ever wondered why the world hates those who come to believe in Jesus the Christ. Have you ever wondered why there can be free speech about anything at all except when that free speech declares that there is something called truth, and that truth will make you free, and everything else is a lie.

Have you ever wondered why you can take the name of the Lord God, and you can take the name of Jesus and abuse them and say whatever you want about them, but you dare not take the name of some other god or prophet or teacher. At the beginning, God declared, there is and always will be a curse upon the enemy of souls, all who relate to that father of lies and the living Christ and all those who belong to Him. There is no place of agreement.

Just in case He has not been clear enough, God then adds something more about the enmity between them and the seed of the woman. Technically, it's known as the Proto-evangelium. The word 'proto' speaks of the 'first' or 'original' thing. The word 'evangelium' is the word which means 'good news'. It is the first glimmer of hope. God tells the serpent that the coming seed of the woman, her offspring; will bruise his head, and that the serpent will bruise the heel of that seed.

God declares right there with the first ever sin mankind committed there would be a child coming from the woman. He says the enemy of souls would manage to bruise the heel of this child. The heel where the lowest part of that seed touches the earth. At the same time that coming person will crush the head of the serpent under their foot.

God said there is a Saviour on the way, who is going to put everything right once more. The serpent has no answer for God then, and still has no answer to the wonder and truth of the good news of Jesus the Christ, who though He was put to death upon a cross, bruised where He walked on the earth, yet He has crushed the power and the hold of the serpent on mankind, by destroying death and the one who held the power of death, even the devil.

Having pronounced the coming of hope and salvation God turns back to the woman, and then to Adam. He still does not pronounce a curse upon them. He now speaks instead to the consequences of their actions. He tells the woman, the result of her action is to bring pain and sorrow into the world, because sin always brings pain and sorrow in the end.

Then He adds this truth, that what she desires will tend to govern her life. I do not know even here that God is making a comment on her gender. I think it is more likely that God is still making a comment on sin. Sin will bring pain and sorrow into a life and the sin we desire will tend to govern our life, and the power of that desire we will often struggle with every day of our life on this earth.

Next God addressed the man and declared that sin would bring consequences to his life also. Adam is going to discover hardship, struggles and sweat. Adam will also know, pain and sorrow. And what he desires will also tend to govern his days. Pain has come into life, thorns and briars will be a struggle for all his days. Here again I am tempted to think God is not merely talking about the weeds which grow in the ground. There are thorns, things that will hurt and scar; briars, things that will cause pain and sorrow in life as we go about trying to live and walk in obedience to all God tells us to do.

God then adds that the mud mankind was made from, mankind will discover in time it will return to the mud they came from. Our existence on the face of the ground is now to be time limited, and then the mud part of us, will become just dirt once more.

The next thing we read is that Adam calls his wife, Eve. There is no record of any conversation they have had up to this point. We do not know if he has ever spoken to her before. It certainly appears that he had never named her up to this point. She was just the part which had come from the man.

Here though Adam now talks to his wife, and says he is going to call her Eve, because she is the mother of all living, or the mother of the life giver.

God has just said there is to be enmity, but He has also pronounced a glimmer of hope. God pronounced pain and sorrow, struggle and difficulty as the result of their sin, but He also declared the truth of a Saviour coming, and Adam heard the voice of God say that and now declares that he will return and do what God had made him to do, despite the pain and the struggle. The man says, "You know what? God told me originally, before I messed up, we would fill the Earth, and He would prosper us and give us life. We have messed up, but God has spoken again, and I believe we can still do what He told me to do, we can still do something that is right and God can still use us to bring the life giver He has promised into this world."

Adam turns to the woman and calls her the one who will now fulfil the declaration of God and bring hope and life, where the two of them had brought only shame, death and despair. He realised that God had still come looking for them. God had still called to them, God was still speaking to them, and in all God said was the declaration of a promise of life and hope.

God then does another work of grace for both the man and the woman. He looked at the way they had sought to cover up their shame and their nakedness, and declared that what they had done, would never be enough to deal with their naked shame. He removed the fig leaves, after all the fig leaves would dry out, shrivel up and never be enough to cover them. In the briefest of moments, what they did had seemed as though it might cover them, but they would quickly discover the fragility and imperfection of their efforts to cover up the results of their sin. Having removed the fig leaves, God made them a garment of skin and then covered them.

Most of the commentators say this was the first ever sacrifice. They say that, because the only way you can get skin from an animal, is to kill it. The revelation is that God takes an animal, and slays that animal, in order to obtain a covering to deal with the guilt and shame of the sin of man and woman. The life of another, given to handle the guilt and shame of the sinner. It is a further declaration of this proto-evangelium, of the death of another, in our place, to deal with the guilt and shame we have for the actions we take in deliberate defiance of the God who made us.

Every time we try and cover our deceit ourselves, we fail. Ultimately our sin and shame will be exposed. But when we confess our sin to a living God, He declares, He has found a covering to deal with the guilt and shame of our naked disobedience.

The story which declares the varied responses to the sin of this first couple, shows the way we still seek to run from God, but above all, it shows the truth of the hope found in a God who is holy, but who comes looking to restore relationship with those who have done wrong, of the way He still calls and speaks to us in spite of our sin, and of His grace and mercy in sending a seed to crush the power of the enemy and create for us a covering for our guilt and shame, that we might still stand before this Holy God, and know Him to be our hope, our joy and our life.

Out of Eden

As you arrive at the last three verses of the third chapter of Genesis, the scene changes significantly. The serpent has left the stage. Adam and Eve have moved back into the garden, and a conversation takes place without any of those three being involved. It is an altogether interesting conversation, adding to truths, so far only seen in the background, and setting out other truths which will significantly change the whole of the Bible story through to the very end.

Whenever we read the Bible, we should always read it, thinking about what it says, but also be aware of what it does not say. We should read it thoughtfully and we are entitled to ask questions of the words which are used. We need to learn to ask questions both about what is actually said and also of the white space, of what it implies but does not actually spell out. In the words recorded in Scripture there is always enough written for us to grasp more than just the obvious meaning of the words.

Verse 22 is a very good example of this, because it records the conversation in this way:

> *Then the LORD God said, "Behold, the man has become like one of us in knowing good and evil.*

Halfway through that sentence is a statement which births a legitimate question, "Who is the US?". It is a reasonable question to say who are the 'us' involved in the conversation.

Commentators offer all sorts of options here. Some suggest that God is here speaking to the heavenly host, the angelic creatures. But nowhere in the scripture does God ever reveal himself to be like an angel. In fact, God is always revealed as altogether different and superior to the angels.

Quite apart from that, there is a further problem with suggesting this refers to the angelic host. It must be noted that all the verbs used in this verse are used in the singular. Only the noun is plural. In all ordinary languages this would be a grammatical error, because you would never put a plural noun with a singular form of the verb. That would be like saying "we am seeing". You would not say that. It should either be "I am" or "We are". But here in the twenty second verse, that is exactly how the noun and verb appear. It leaves us then asking still, "Who is the Us who am talking here?".

Genesis, remember, is a book of beginnings. It is a revelation of the living God which begins here and will continue right the way through the scripture. So it is that in the very beginning here as in chapter one we are being introduced to a mystery of the Lord our God who is one God, and yet He speaks in ways that suggest more than one person is present. We are being reminded here, of truths hinted at in that first chapter of the God, who created by means of His Word, and the activity of the Holy Spirit who even there was moving. For the scripture will take these early hints and slowly reveal more of the mystery of the triune majesty on high, one God in three distinct persons.

Even more significant are the words the one God uses. He says that the man has become like 'one of us'. Notice He does not say the man has become 'like us' but rather He declares 'like one of us'. Just as we asked, who are the 'us', we have the right to ask why it speaks of 'one of us' and not just of 'us'.

This is another legitimate question. It asks whether we are being told that the man has become godlike, or is there something different beginning to be revealed here?

It is especially significant since chapter one taught that man was created in the image and likeness of God. We noticed those words do not begin to suggest that man was created to be the same as God, although there are some characteristics which man originally had which were similar to what is true about God, but man will never be the same as the eternally unchanging, altogether holy, all powerful, omniscient, ever present God. That is just to mention a few of the characteristics of the eternal Godhead which we will never replicate. Nor do these words in the third chapter suggest any of that is changed at all.

So a legitimate question to ask is this, 'in what way has the man changed so that God can declare "the man has become like one of us"'? The verse itself gives an answer to that question when it declares "knowing good and evil." There is something which has changed in the nature of the man in terms of his knowing good and evil. The couple have eaten the fruit of a tree. It was not an apple tree. Nowhere does it suggest that it was an apple tree. It was the tree of the knowledge of good and evil. The woman was deceived by the serpent who came along and said, "God knows the day you eat from that tree, you'll be like God, you will know the difference between good and evil." Now there is a sense in which, what he said was true, though he hid the nature of the consequences of disobeying God. The sense in which it was true is this. The day they ate, everything changed. They now know good and evil, they understand the difference between right and wrong. They have an intimate awareness of good and evil. They have a complete understanding of what it was to do that which was right and that which was wrong.

Up until they took and ate the fruit, they had just been living in the sweetness and favour of God. They had never done anything wrong in thought word or action. However long they had been around, until they ate they did not understand the difference between being good and being evil. The moment they chose to disobey God they understood intimately and completely, the difference between doing the right thing and doing the wrong thing. From that moment on, they are always going to struggle to do the right thing again.

That is why you never need to teach a child to do something they should not. It is one of the proofs of this narrative. All our life we never need to be shown how to misbehave and do wrong. Somebody has to teach us what it is to do right. All the time we have an intimate awareness of what the difference is. God, on the other hand, is only good. Everything about him is good. Everything He does, everything He thinks, everything He feels, is good, and it is good all the time. He has such an awareness of what is good to the point that He understands that anything outside of His will is bad.

When the couple eat, God comes and declares that since the man has done something wrong, he now has an understanding of what God knows, there is a difference between right and wrong. The triune God knows this from the perspective of only ever doing what is good and right. Man, on the other hand now understands it solely from the perspective of doing something wrong.

Then God continues the discussion He is having within the trinity by addressing, for our benefit, the situation which now faces Him. If he allows the couple to live like that and then go on to eat the fruit of the tree of life, the couple and all who flow from them will always and only know the result of doing wrong in the outworking of misery, shame, fear, pain and sorrow. In order to stop that being the only future possible for mankind, God declares He needs to do something to keep the couple from eating the fruit of this second tree in the centre of the garden, which had so far never been touched. To ensure the man does not take pain, sorrow, misery, wickedness, and evil, and make that something they can never, ever lose, God explains His design, to exclude mankind from this tree and from the garden.

Understand what is being done here, because if you are not careful you can read it in a way which makes God look harsh. Whereas the truth is, He does what He does because he loves us. He loves us so much, He does not want to leave us in pain, misery, sorrow, despair and shame, for eternity. He wants to reach us and touch us, and still bring us to the fullness of the hope He has hinted at in the words He spoke to the woman.

God says, "we need to send man out of the garden, we need to remove him from being able to do something which will leave him in hopelessness and despair for ever. We will send him out of the garden and we will send him out of the garden with a job. Man will work the ground." King James says "till the ground."

The word translated 'till' or 'work' in verse 23, is a word which simply means to be occupied. God is not saying we will all be farmers, but that His plan is for humanity to be gainfully occupied. That occupation is going to be different to what it was before man did wrong. It is going to be hard. It is going to be graft. It is going to be laborious. It is going to mean we are going to sweat and strain. Recognise God does not say we are not intended to enjoy it, but He does say, it is going to be laborious. We are going to have to work for our living.

This Hebrew word translated 'till' or 'work' does not just speak of gainful occupation. It can also be translated by the word "serve". It suggests that we are meant to work and that gainful occupation will also include learning to serve. It also has the idea behind it that whatever we do, we should realise we are never in complete control of our destiny. We are always in the hands of something or someone else.

When God made man, He made him, and gave him complete dominion and authority over what he would do. It was a delegated authority, authority under God, but authority to choose what and when to act. When man sinned he gave up that dominion and authority by acting in obedience to the words of the serpent. He chose to place himself under the dominion and authority of the evil one, in that moment he lost the power to control his destiny. Now God says, man will learn to serve, and he will occupy himself by serving the dust. He will work on the ground as a permanent reminder that he is made from mud, dirt, dust. As we work and serve the earth, it should remind us that having been made from dust, we will soon return to dust, ashes to ashes, dust to dust. We should remember our days on this earth are limited.

Alexander the Great, one of the greatest soldiers of his time, employed one soldier whose had a particular task. Every day he had to break into the schedule of his master. He was not to do this at the same time every day. He was not to take account of anything else that Alexander was engaged in. At some time every day he had to come into the presence of his master and say, 'Alexander, remember you will die.'

God said "I'm going to put man out of reach of the tree of life, and I need him to remember his destiny is not in his hands, and he is mortal." So God drove the man and the woman out of the garden. It suggests He actually pushed them out. He pushed them out towards the East.

The verses then tells us that God did two other things. He placed two elements at the entry to the garden to ensure the man could never make his own way back and gain access to the tree of life. They are two separate elements God does. First He placed cherubim at the entry to the garden. All too often we fail to understand the nature of these creatures. We tend to mess up the word and speak of babies and infants as little cherubs. That is a huge mistake for it minimises our understanding of their power and abilities. As far as we can tell, the cherubim are creatures with multiple faces. They are able to face in every direction at the same time. They have eyes that see everything and they move either at the speed of light or faster and are like burning coals of fire.

He put cherubim there and their job was to guard and keep the tree of life secure. Their role was to ensure man would never get back to the garden on their own terms. They ensure mankind could not return to the garden unless they could gain access past these angelic creatures, who see everything, could move everywhere and understand the holiness and purity of the living God.

The second thing God placed at the entrance back into the garden, was a sword of flame. Some commentators suggest the sword was in the hands of the cherubim, but the text does not say that. It says this was a second thing placed there. This is a sword of fire which is turning in all directions. The role of this sword is to ensure that the absolute holiness and perfection of God is never breached by a man gaining his own access into the garden to eat of the tree of Life. The sword turns in every direction.

Man has exited eastward, but the cherubim guards and the sword which turns in every direction are both there to ensure we can never gain our own access to this tree of life.

The tree of life, speaks of the source of life, and the fruit of that tree speaks of the ability to gain access to an abundant life, an existence filled by the absolute and never ending sweetness of the presence of God, of His blessing and favour resting upon an individual as they are. That was now to be kept from man in his state of intimate understanding of disobedience and evil.

This tree of life is described not only at the start of this book of beginnings, we find it is mentioned again in the last book of the scripture, in the Revelation of Jesus the Christ and in the twenty fourth chapter. There we discover there are those who have now gained free access to this tree of life. In Genesis everyone is excluded. In Revelation some have been granted access. There we are told those who have access to the tree of life, are the ones who have been cleansed of all their errors and faults.

The tree of life is also spoken about in the book of Proverbs, and there, in the third chapter, it tells us that wisdom is a tree of life, and those who hold on to wisdom will get back to the tree of life and know the blessing and favour of the living God upon them. It declares our need for wisdom. Then it begins to describe exactly what it means by wisdom. It does that through the next few chapters, right up to and through chapter eight.

Reading through those chapters, you begin to comprehend this description of wisdom is not just speaking of an abstract understanding, but rather it is speaking of a person. It speaks of one who was with the father before the creation of the world. It speaks about a wisdom which is made manifest in a person who is coming into the world. It begins to unpack the wonder of the Lord Jesus Christ, who is there in eternity, and from eternity to eternity, yet broke into time at Bethlehem's manger and was born as a man and walked upon the face of the Earth. The same one who went to a cross, died and rose again to life. That cross becomes not only the tree of His death but also becomes the tree of life to all who put their trust and hope in Him. To them it becomes the place of cleansing, of the removal of all faults and sins, and the way of restoration of the fullness of fellowship in the presence of the triune God.

The sword that was placed there, that flaming sword of the holiness of God and of His wrath against evil is also to be dealt with in the scripture. Zechariah the prophet hears from the mouth of God and in the twelfth verse of the thirteenth chapter he is told that the sword of God has struck the one who stands by the father, the shepherd of the Bible, the great shepherd of the sheep. The wrath of God's purity and holiness has struck down the Saviour, Jesus the Christ, in order that the flame might be quenched, God's holy wrath satisfied, and access back to the wonder of abundant life regained.

The sword of God's wrath fell on the saviour on Calvary's tree when He carried our sin and our shame, when He took our guilt and bore our curse. As the weight of the sin of man was laid upon his shoulders, that sword fell on Him. Through His sacrifice and righteousness, a way to come and find a life free from curse, free from the power of evil, free from the guilt and shame of sin and a life walking in the blessing of God, with the presence and friendship of God was once more opened.

Reading the end of Genesis chapter three, and realising the man and the woman have been driven out of the garden, away from the tree of life, may leave us thinking their was no hope, and no way out of a world of despair and misery. But the next thing we read at the start of chapter four, is that Adam knew His wife. That word 'know' means he had an intimate understanding of where she was at, what her problems were, what she had bought into his life, what she could do for the world. Eve became pregnant and gave birth and immediately she cries out and says "Look the seed God promised has come." Actually she missed it because this babe was Cain. But she knew and Adam knew, they had been driven out, kept away from the tree of life, but they were hanging on to a promise from God that they would once more gain access back to the presence of the living God through the coming seed who would crush the sting of death and the one who had the power of death, the devil. They were driven out, but they lived in the hope and promise that God would not drive away for ever.

We read these words with the understanding that we may still go through some more pain, we may make yet more messes in our lives, we may still go astray, we may wander and struggle, we may still do and see other things that are wrong, sinful, evil, but that need not be the end of our story. God wanted the first couple to know, but also wants us to know He has yet more to reveal of the wonder of His love, the wonder of His mercy, the wonder of His grace, the wonder of His salvation, the wonder of His life giving power, His wisdom and His understanding that in a world of sin, we might still live in hope and faith.

God drove them out from His presence, but He drove them out with a promise, that reflected the love and value He has towards mankind. He sees us as so valuable, so precious that He does all He can to keep us from living in eternal death and instead offer to all of us a way to eternal life found in the tree of Calvary, the tree of life, the tree whose leaves are for the healing of the all ethnicities who trust in Him.

Children in the family

Many things change between Chapter three and four of this book of beginnings. There is a transition here, not just a chapter break in our Bibles. It is a significant transition for the couple because they have been expelled from the garden of Eden, driven out from the place where God met with them, excluded from the place with easy access into His presence, sent out from the place of communion and fellowship with Him. Chapter four finds them in a very different place. There is also about to be a further transition. The man and the woman will move from being a couple into becoming a family. They are about to bring a baby into the world, with all this will mean in changes to the way they have lived up to this point. Both of those, are massive transitions.

Nothing fully prepares a couple for the arrival of children into a home. This first couple are in this period of transition. It all causes then to live and experience many significant changes taking place in their lives together.

Many questions may occur to us as we come to this portion. A number of those questions are suggested by the text, some relate to what is omitted from the text. Many of these questions are not spelt out. Some of them are just implied. Some of the answers are implied. Some of the questions are just left hanging with no attempt to give any clear answer. When we come to the word of God and are left with unanswered questions, there need be nothing implicitly wrong with asking them, as long as any answer we give or suggest is in line with the whole body of scripture teaching.

One of the questions I wonder about is this. They have been driven out of the garden, how far did they move away from the garden? What distance did they have to go? We are not told or even given a clue. The implication is they did not travel far from the garden since when they were driven out, the cherubim and the sword of flame were put at the entrance to stop them going back into the garden. So the implication is, they were not far away from the entrance to the garden. But it is a legitimate question. How far were they driven? How far did they go at the beginning? We are told that as the family grew they went further and further from the garden. But at the start, we just do not know how close they stayed to the guarded entrance.

The implication is that they did not travel far from the outside of the gate. If that is true, not only did they live every day with the knowledge of what they lost, but also in sight of and with that constant reminder of what they had lost. What does that knowledge do to a couple? What does it do to a family? What does it do in a relationship when you live with a permanent reminder of the consequences of your wrong doing.

What kind of family were those children going to be born into? Did they live so close to the garden, that every morning they got up, looked out, and there was the reminder of what they had been excluded from. Every day as they went about their trials, every evening when they went to bed, were they close enough to be reminded of the result of their sin.

Have you ever lived with the consequences of what you have done wrong? There they are, staring you in the face every day. It does things to your mind, your life, your relationships.

Remember this mud couple, were created with limitations, with flaws. They were created, but there was something missing which made them less than good, until they were brought together. God created man with the need for somebody else. This family that was created good now looks as though it is on shaky ground, and the children have not even arrived yet. Turning to read Genesis four, those kind of questions arise and are left unanswered.

The first sentence of chapter four tells us that Adam knew Eve, his wife and she conceived and she bore Cain. How long had they lived outside the garden before that happened? How long had they lived with the reminder of what they had done wrong, before things moved on? We are not given any clues as to the time span. All we know is that things have moved on, and one of the ways in which they have moved on is this. Adam knew his wife, Eve, she conceived and bore Cain.

In some of the translations it says and Adam made love to Eve, his wife. I do not know whether there was any love there between them at this time. There certainly is no mention of love in the Hebrew. In one of the translations, it says Adam had sexual relations with Eve, his wife. But the Hebrew word says Adam 'knew' his wife. It is this word which speaks of intimate knowledge and understanding. It certainly includes physical intimacy. But it really includes far more than that. This word 'knew' involves an emotional and an intellectual response, based on information received, analysed and worked out.

That is worth stopping and thinking about. It speaks of physical intimacy being a part of an emotional and intellectual response to information received, analysed and worked on. It is worth noticing because we live in a world where people engage in sexual activity without even stopping to think about whether they know each other in these terms.

All day, every day, we live in a world which would suggest that any real emotional and intellectual response is an unnecessary encumbrance when it comes to sexual activity. The world chooses to glorify and magnify the mere physicality of the action. It is, after all a physical act, but being involved in physical intimacy will always involve an emotional and intellectual response. You cannot be sexually intimate in a vacuum.

This word 'know' suggests they had an emotional and intellectual awareness of one another. When did that take place, when did they get to 'know' each other? Was it, when he first saw and said 'flesh of my flesh and bone of my bone'? Was it when they were told that they were to cleave to one another?

Some people suggest that the whole purpose of dating is about getting data, about getting information, and no more. What did Adam know about Eve? That is a legitimate question. The name Eve, and it is interesting because it does not say and 'Adam knew his wife', it says, and 'Adam knew Eve, his wife. It draws attention to the fact that Adam knew that Eve was his wife. He only had one wife. We are told Adam had an emotional and intellectual knowledge based on an analysis of data received and experience shared, that his wife was Eve.

The Bible is written in three different languages. Most of the Old Testament is written in Hebrew, the majority of the New Testament is written in Greek, and then there are some parts of the Bible written in Aramaic. The Old Testament is written in Hebrew and in Aramaic. It is normally reckoned that one of the oldest languages in the world is Aramaic. It is the language that Jesus spoke.

We know that the name 'Eve' in Hebrew means the mother of all living. In Aramaic, that same name 'Eve' comes from the word 'serpent'. Did Adam get up every morning and greet his wife as the 'mother of all living', or did he come to her and always refer to her as 'the snake', 'the serpent'? Did he live in sight of all they had lost, and carry on blaming her?

If he woke every morning and went through the day refering to her as the serpent, the cause of their exclusion, the one he blamed for their situation, what kind of family were the children born into? We are not told, we have no idea what was going on within the home. All we are told is that Adam new Eve, his wife and she conceived.

The verse says that Adam knew Eve, his wife and she conceived and gave birth to Cain. Some of that sentence is almost superfluous. For her to bear a child, she had to conceive, and to conceive she had to have engaged in sexual intimacy. It is that unnecessary detail which makes me suggest that knowing her means far more than just saying he was acquainted with her or simply, that they made love.

Then the verse tells us that after she conceived, she bore Cain. She bore the child and she named him Cain and then explains, the child is to be called Cain because she got this man from the Lord. She looked at the baby and said 'he is the man from the Lord'. The name Cain means 'acquired', 'got from', 'possessed by'. So she bore a son, and said, 'This is the one I have got and acquired from God, the one who is possessed as the man from the Lord.

That would mean Cain would grow up, with expectations put upon him by his family. Eve said he was the one, the man that she had got from God. He would grow up with the expectation his parents have, put on him every moment he is awake. His name will always remind him that his mother believed he was the one who would fix everything.

Then in verse two his brother Abel arrives. The way it is put in the Hebrew, says something like this 'again she bore his brother Abel'. There is no mention of Adam knowing Eve, no mention of the conception, no special reason given for his name, just 'Abel came'. The word Abel comes from the Hebrew word for 'vapour' or maybe a sigh. The implication is she gave birth and after giving birth she sighed, she let her breath out, and the sigh was what they called this second son.

How long it was between the birth of Cain and Abel being born? We are not told, all it says is 'later' Abel came along. How long did Cain live with the expectation of his parents on him as an only child? As an only child, did he feel special? He would have felt special as the one who came from God, with God upon his life, and then at some time later, he ceased to be an only son and this 'sigh' person came along.

Cain may have grown up for some time as the center of the family, as well as having expectation of his parents upon him, but when Abel turned up, no reason is given for the name of this second child. According to the text, whenever this second son is mentioned, he is referred to as 'Abel, Cain's brother'. Abel came along and appears to live his life in the shadow of his older brother.

There is no reference to their childhood, no comment on them growing up. There is no reference to what the family looked like. There is no further comment on the family life until we discover that both sons have started to work. I wonder what went on in that family with those boys.

Whatever went on there is no comment until we discover them working and Abel is keeping sheep while Cain is working on the land.

That is important information. Because you are told Cain is given the job of following in his father's footsteps. God had given Adam the task of looking after the ground. That role is now being passed on to Cain. Every day Abel is looking after animals, while Cain goes off to work with his father, on the land. Cain is going to learn what to do from watching his father and doing the same. Abel is just there to look out for the sheep.

Family struggles will go on right the way down through the scriptures between the older brother and the next brother. Rivalries are set up not just within this family but in other families over and over again. It is too easy to set up rivalries between the children. I wonder if that rivalry was down to a rivalry between Adam and Eve, between husband and wife. A rivalry that will then play out between the children.

Whatever interaction there was in each of those relationships is hidden from us, but is existing some time during verse two. Then we read in the third verse:

> *In the course of time Cain brought to the LORD
> an offering of the fruit of the ground,*

Time has passed somewhere between verse two and three. Some time later, 'in the course of time' Cain came and brought an offering of the fruit of the ground. He brought this as an offering unto the LORD. It was a personal offering.

Then the fourth verse reads:

> *and Abel also brought of the firstborn of his flock*

> *and of their fat portions. And the LORD had*
> *regard for Abel and his offering, but for Cain and*
> *his offering he had no regard. So Cain was very*
> *angry, and his face fell.*   *Genesis 4:4-5*

Abel also brought a part of the first born of his flock. Understand we are being told in these verses that both the boys brought an offering. Both boys brought an offering using elements connected with their role in life. Cain looked after the ground and brought an offering of the fruit of the ground. Abel looked after the animals and brought an offering from among the animals.

All the way through the scripture, the words 'brought' and 'offering' are used in relation to worship. We are being told that both the boys came to worship. As they came to worship they desired to offer something as worship to the LORD.

The implication is, and it is confirmed elsewhere in the scripture, Adam has taken the time to tell them about God. It suggests Adam told them about the garden. He probably told them about the flaming sword and the cherubim, about the purpose of those two things. He probably explained their parents exclusion from the garden. He would have told them his story. He would have spoken of the judgment which had fallen on the couple because of sin and of the promise of a man who would solve the problem of death and their exclusion from the presence of God.

Adam must have spoken of the need to worship, because both Cain and Abel came to worship. They both came to worship, bringing an offering. They came bringing a gift of worship to the living God. Both came expecting that when they walked into the presence of God with their offering and their worship, God would accept what they brought.

We are specifically told that the Lord had respect unto Abel's offering but He had no regard for Cain's offering. There was no way God looked on the one but did not look on the other. He looked on them both, but as He looked on one, He had 'respect' for it but had no 'regard' for the other when He saw it. The Hebrew text is best translated by saying 'He looked favourably' on Abel's offering but 'He turned away from gazing' at Cain's offering.

That provokes a question, and finding the right answer to it is significant if we are wanting to come before God in worship with the desire and intention that He will look favourably upon what we bring to Him. We have to ask why the offering Abel brought found favour in the sight of God but the offering Cain brought caused God to look away.

There are two clues in the text which suggest the answer to finding favour with God as we bring our worship to offer unto Him. The first clue is about time. The second clue is about intention.

The third verse says Cain came "in the process of time", he came after a while. The words suggest Cain came to God "when it was convenient," he came after he had done everything else he wanted to do first. He came eventually. It suggests coming to worship was not a priority to Cain, but an optional element. He sought to worship as long as he could find the time to fit it into his busy schedule.

Then it says that he brought an offering of the fruit of the ground. The term 'of the fruit' uses a Hebrew word which suggests he brought 'some of what was left over'.

Both those things together suggest Cain came to worship when he could find time to fit it in and then he brought as his worship what was left over, what he felt he could spare. If that is true, Cain worshipped when he had nothing else he could think of doing and he brought to God, what was left over after he had taken what he needed. He has lived with the expectation of God doing something special with him, but chose to live a life where God took second place.

Abel did everything differently. We are told that Abel comes and he brings the firstborn and he brings the fat. We need to understand, the significance of this. When the first animal gave birth, before Abel did anything else, and not knowing whether another animal would follow, he brought the first to God. Then it says 'he brought the fat'. The fat speaks of what is the very best, that which is the most desireable. The whole offering Abel brought, said that God had the first place in his attention and deserved the very best which Abel could bring as an offering.

The result was that the Lord had regard to Abel, and to his offering. God had regard both for the person bringing the offering and the offering itself. God looked on Abel with favour and with pleasure. Then having looked on Abel like that, He also looked at the offering Abel brought, with favour and with pleasure.

Watch the sequence of the text. God looked at the offerer first and then at the offering they brought. He looked at Cain without favour or pleasure, and then He looked at Cain's offering without any favour or pleasure. Cain brought what was left over, when he had time to spare. He looked at Abel with favour and then saw the offering brought and regarded that also with favour. Abel brought his best and first to God.

The issue of what comes first in the priorities of life and what we do with our very best is always a matter of the heart.

Cain came to God expecting that if he bought something, anything as an offering, God would bless him anyway. Abel came not knowing whether God would do anything for him or not, but recognising that whether God blessed Him or not, God was still worthy of the very best he could bring. God deserves the best and He deserves what we offer to Him, to be a recognition that in all we are and all we have He has the first place in our lives.

How we come to worship, the attitude of our hearts and the place we give to God in all of our life will change the result of the worship we offer and the response we receive from the living God. He deserves the highest place, the first priority, the fullest praise, just because He is God.

Verse five then tells us that when Cain saw God was not pleased with him or his offering, he was very angry. The Hebrew text says Cain 'burned with rage'. He was angry. He was livid, because he had brought something to God, he had come to worship God and he believed God ought to look on him and be grateful. Cain was angry, and then the text continues and says 'his face fell'.

Cain found himself at that moment in the place of worship, in the presence of God, angry, burning with rage, livid. He was angry because he had not received the response he thought God ought to give him. Then that anger caused his face to fall. It means he looked downcast and miserable. In the presence of God, in the place of worship Cain was angry and miserable.

The next thing we read is that God says something to him. That means Cain must have still been there before God. He must have been standing in the presence of God, angry, livid and miserable. In the sight of the God who had made him and watched over his life, Cain was angry and miserable, eaten up with rage.

The amazing truth is, even though Cain was furious and miserable, cross with God, and refusing to look at God, the matchless love and kindness of God still chose to speak to him.

> *The LORD said to Cain, "Why are you angry, and why has your face fallen? If you do well, will you not be accepted? And if you do not do well, sin is crouching at the door. Its desire is contrary to you, but you must rule over it."* Genesis 4:6-7

God spoke to Cain and asked him to think about what was making him angry and miserable. He asked Cain to consider what was winding him up so much and why it had happened.

Reading the story I wonder whether Cain was cross and miserable just because God had not accepted him or his offering? It may also have been the case that he was angry about the way God had accepted his brother and his offering. Was he angry over what he had not received, or was he just as angry that someone else had received the favour and pleasure of God? Was it that the other person, was his younger brother? Did Cain believe Abel did not deserve to get favour from God? What was it that was eating Cain up and moved him from just burning with rage, to becoming miserable and downcast? What is it which irritates most, the fact that God does not do for us what we expect Him to do, or the fact that God has sometimes does it for somebody else?

God asked him to think about the person and sacrifice which was not accepted, and then to recognise the difference between his offering and his brother's offering. Then in loving kindness God tells Cain if he then goes and does what is right and offer to God the first and the best of his life, he can find he also will be accepted.

It is the mercy and grace of God which comes to us when we have done something not pleasing to Him, that He invites us to think about our error, to change what we do, and come again to worship and offer to him an acceptable sacrifice of praise.

Have you ever been angry with God? It is so easy to be in the place of worship, with a heart still churning, because God did not do what we thought he should do for us, and He did it for somebody else, and we believe we are at least as deserving as them.

God regularly explains, He does not need to tell any of us what He is doing or why He is doing it. He just requires us to remember and know that He is God. We come and worship out of a heart that recognises Him for who He is, and that He is able to do whatever He chooses to do, and whatever that means for us we will still worship and offer to Him our best.

Cain was angry with God, because he did not think God had dealt fairly with him. I confess to recognising that feeling and emotion. I know what it is to be in the place of worship with my hands raised, angry, because I believe what has happened to me should never have been allowed to happen. It was not fair. I did my best, and things still did not work out the way I believed they should. I have had things go wrong, while other people seem to have received better treatment than me.

In times like this God says 'Why are you angry? Will you not just trust me and worship out of a heart that brings your best, no matter what because I am God and all I am doing will work out for My glory and your best in the end?'

'Choose to do right'

> *In the course of time Cain brought to the Lord an offering of the fruit of the ground, and Abel also brought of the firstborn of his flock and of their fat portions. And the Lord had regard for Abel and his offering, but for Cain and his offering he had no regard. So Cain was very angry, and his face fell. The Lord said to Cain, "Why are you angry, and why has your face fallen? If you do well, will you not be accepted? And if you do not do well, sin is crouching at the door. Its desire is contrary to you, but you must rule over it."   Genesis 4:3-7*

With the two brothers, different ages, who have come to bring an offering to God, with the aim of coming to worship this creator God the scene is set for sin to continue to make it's powerful presence known within this first family.

While the offering of one brother was received by God the other was not. It was not received by God because the thinking and the heart of Cain was wrong, and this living God is being revealed as the God who looks on the heart and weighs the motives and the intentions of those who come before Him.

Cain thought it was acceptable to worship God on his own terms, and the truth is we can never worship God acceptably on our terms. We worship God on His terms. He is the God who always declares He will have all of our heart, all of our worship, all of our praise, or He will have none of it.

Cain finding his worship has failed to find favour in the sight of God, has began to be angry and miserable then God spoke to him. The words God spoke are recorded for us in verses six and seven and we turn now to further consider those words.

The two verses raise a number of questions. One of the big problems we have as we read these words is about not knowing the tone of God's voice as He spoke to Cain. We do not know entirely what God was thinking, what His heart wanted to convey in the words He chose to speak. We can have a guess, but we really do not know.

For example when God said, 'Why are you angry? Why is your countenance fallen? Was His tone one of innocent inquiry, or did it convey a sense of indignation, or could His tone have implied something else entirely?

Not only are we unaware of the tone of God's voice, but equally we do not know how Cain heard these words. It can often be the case, when somebody speaks to us that how we hear and interpret their words can be deeply affected by whatever is going on in our life at that moment. What they say could be said and meant in total innocence but because of the way we are thinking and feeling it can be met with a sharp or sarcastic response.

We do not know God's tone or His intention, nor do we know how Cain heard what was said. All we can really be certain of is this. God spoke to Cain. We can also be sure that when God spoke these words to Cain, recorded in verses six and seven, He had one absolute object in mind. He wanted to stop Cain coming to the place where the actions recorded from verse eight would take place.

If you mark your Bible, you might want to put a line between verse seven and eight. There ought to be a chapter break there. Certainly there is a break in time. How long it was between the words God spoke to Cain, and then Cain speaking to his brother and setting in motion the actions which follow, we do not know. We just know there was a gap, a break in time.

But God's intention in speaking to Cain was to seek to keep him from coming to the actions which unfold from verse eight.

One of the problems we have as we read what God is recorded as saying in verses six and seven, is that we know what happens next. But just for a while, try to put that knowledge from your mind and try to think just about the recorded words of God to Cain in these two verses.

God asked two questions. Those two questions appear to have two totally distinct purposes. The first question is "why are you angry?" God asks this question and the object behind it is "Why are you mad with me?" Then God asks, "Why is your face fallen?" The word translated by this phrase 'face fell' has to do with the idea of envy and jealousy. So the second question is really about relationship with Abel his brother.

God is asking Cain to think first about how he views God, and about his relationship with God. Then God asks him to think about his brother, Abel.

One of the issues we face is realising that this seventh verse is one of the most difficult verses in the whole of the Old Testament to translate and interpret. It is difficult because it uses words which have a number of different meanings. There are forms in the way that Hebrew is written which mean we are not sure exactly which words in this verse are the object of a verb and which are the subjects.

On top of that, there are words, added in English, which are not in the original text. If you use a good english translation those words are written in italics to indicate they are absent in the original and have been added to try to make sense of the possible meaning of the words which do appear.

This seventh verse is one of those verses where things are implied, but never fully clarified. We will try over these next few pages to give understanding and meaning to that verse, but know that other good commentators may take a different view and may even be justified in doing so. For all of that I believe it has some powerful revelations we ought to stop, wrestle with and think about.

God asks Cain why he is angry and why his countenance has fallen. Then God makes a statement. In that sentence God asks two questions followed by a statement. God raises these questions, and then makes His statement. One of the things that is fascinating is that while God speaks and asks these two questions and makes this statement, there appears to be no response to either questions from Cain. Certainly none is recorded. It is implied that Cain is absolutely silent, and just stands in front of God, in this place of worship, with his head down with nothing to say to God.

Often the first time we know somebody is angry with us is when they stop talking to us. The next clue to somebody being angry with us is when they not only have nothing to say to us, but they refuse to even look at us.

The thing that is incredible is Cain never appears to utter a word in response to the questions and more than that he never even looks at the God he had come to worship. Yet God still speaks to Cain. God initiates this conversation. He knows how angry Cain is. God understands Cain is angry, and He recognises the anger is because of the response he received from God, to his offering. It was not the response Cain had expected.

So he is angry with God. On top of that he is jealous because of the response his brother has received from God. Cain is envious of his brother. Cain is there, like that, and God is still speaking to him. Cain says, not a word. God comes and asks a question and Cain says nothing. God asks another question, and still Cain says nothing. But God still carries on talking to Cain trying to engage with Cain.

I do not know if you have ever done something and finished up not ready to talk to God. Maybe you have never even got to the stage of wanting to talk to God. This verse, indeed the whole of the scripture tells us, God has something to say to each of us. God is still speaking whatever our response. He is the God who always speaks and He speaks in order to reach out to us, in order to speak into our life to change our life for the better.

After asking the two questions, God makes a statement. He says "if you do well you would be accepted". It implies that even though Cain may be in the wrong place at the moment God wants him to know it is still possible to change. God comes and tells Cain he may think God has written him off, now, but that is not true. This living God is the God not just of a second chance but of another chance.

There was a stage in my life when I was tempted to join a particular group of churches. I met with one of their senior leaders who told me their view about failings was along the lines of the old baseball statement, 'three strikes and you are out'. He was suggesting they may still accept me into their group, despite my past. His comment was a deal breaker to me. I chose to look elsewhere, because I have messed up in the past. I had already used more than three 'strikes' years ago. I thank God, He is a God who always comes and gives us not just three chances but another chance.

When we look at what God said to Cain, we also need to acknowledge we do not know how Cain heard these words. If somebody comes to you and in all innocence, says to you 'if you would just do the right thing', how do you hear that. You are all churned up with anger, envy and resentment. Did Cain hear God speak and hear it as though God had said "if only you were as good as your brother".

One of the problems we often have in life is a tendency to always view, compare and judge ourselves against the lives and experiences of others. We are checking to see if we are better than, or more acceptable than those around us. Was that Cain's issue and mindset when God spoke to him.

Then the phrase recorded as the words from God have some interesting nuances. As we read it, we would expect it to say 'if you do well, you will be accepted, and if you do not do well'. God never says that. We might expect God to have said 'if you do well, this will happen, but if you do wrong, this will happen', but He does not say that. Instead God comes and tells Cain if he does well, he will find a response from Him, but if he fails to do the right thing there is an outcome but the outcome will involve something which God does not control.

The thing to realise is, God never tells Cain that if he does not do well He will reject him. He comes to Cain as He comes to each of us and says "I want to give you another chance. I want to give you another opportunity to walk the right path, to go the right way, to do the right thing." God's word comes and offers another chance, another opportunity to worship aright. Every chance God gives is an opportunity to make a choice. The choice is extremely simple. The choice is to do right or not to do right. It is not choosing to do right or to do wrong. There is no choice to do wrong. Doing wrong is simply a matter of choosing not to do right, for with God there is a single right path that either we choose to follow or we choose not to follow. Because for God, there is only one right path. He declares, "Give me your heart, give me your soul and give me all of your life." Anything other than that is the choice not to do right.

God comes and says "I have set before you a choice, the opportunity to be blessed. The opportunity is to be where I can touch you and bless you and favour you and speak into your life." The choice is to come to God and be blessed but if you refuse to do right there will be an outcome and a consequence.

God never says He will reject Cain. But what He does say is powerful. He says if Cain chooses to do right he will be favoured and he will not need to live with the failure of what he had done up to this point.

God then adds that if Cain chooses not to do what is right, sin is crouching at the door. The word that is translated 'sin' here is a word which comes from a root that speaks about missing the mark. It is a word that speaks about a target aimed for, but missed. It speaks of a standard failed.

Cain already knew what it was to miss target, to fail to reach the required standard, because he has discovered that in coming to worship God, it was only possible to draw near and offer worship on God's terms.

The verse speaks of 'sin crouching at the door.' It uses a phrase which speaks about an animal crouched, lying at a door. It is a difficult phrase to interpret, because it does not tell you what kind of animal it is. It is difficult because Hebrew uses this word in relation not only to a wild animal, but also when speaking of a pet. So you could read this verse as though it is saying 'if you do not do the right thing, sin is lying like a pet at your door.' Exactly the same word could be read "sin is crouching, ready to pounce like a wild animal. .

It is not clear which of the two, a pet or a wild animal, God is speaking of and likening sin to. Often where a verse of scripture can be read in two different ways, my inclination is to believe God intends us to read both into the text.

If that is the what we do here God might intend us to read these words with the knowledge of having a pet dog which is laying down at the door waiting to see you coming. It has been lying down and it has missed you. As soon as you come through the door, it jumps up, and jumps onto you. The pet looks so sweet, so nice, and as it jumps up at you, you think you can handle this. Like this God intends us to understand, our temptation to look at sin, and think we can handle it. It looks so sweet, so pleasant, it surely will not do us harm.

I can never get over those people who welcome you into their home and they have a dog which is just running around, jumping up to greet you, and they say something like this, "It is alright, he does not bite". Whatever they say I always know the dog has teeth, it bites. It may look sweet. But if you do one thing wrong it is still able to bite you.

Sin crouching like a pet dog is like that. It looks nice. It looks as though we can handle it. We may even think we sinned before and got away with it. We believe we know what we are doing. Yet, the minute we allow sin in, it will have us, it will look to control us. That pet sin we think we can handle will manifest itself in ways that will alter our life without thinking about it.

God comes and says to Cain, sin is crouched at the door, while it looks like a pet, you can handle, in reality it is a wild animal desiring to destroy you. It is crouched waiting to pounce.

Years later the Lord Jesus said to Peter, 'Satan, has desired to have you'. God tells Cain, sin wants to have him. The word 'have' means 'to master', 'to control', 'to own'. Sin wants to master and own him so that he is under it's control, to stop him being able to do anything outside of the control of sin.

God comes and says "It is at the door, Cain. At the moment you are in a place of danger. I know where your heart is at. I know the anger and the envy inside you. I know where that can lead you. If you make the wrong decision, something will die. You will die. A relationship will die. A brother will die. A prospect will die. The plan and purpose for your life will die, if you make the wrong choice. Do not let it, and do not do it."

Sin always wants to master, control and rule over us. The desire of sin is always against our best interests. As God continues to explains all this to Cain, He says "Rather than

143

sin controlling you, you must learn to rule over it."

The implication of what God outlines here, right at the beginning of the revelation of His word, is that whether sin rules us, or we rule sin, is a choice we can make.

Sin is ever waiting at the door of our heart, at the entrance of our mind, seeking access to our will, looking for a way in to our life, waiting to pounce and grab us, to master us. We do not have the strength to overcome it. Sin is crouching at the door, and we cannot overcome it alone, but also standing at the door of our heart, looking for entrance to our mind, and access to our will, is the Lord Jesus Christ. He stands knocking and declares, if we will open the door to Him, He will come in, shut the door, settle down and commune with us. He has the strength to overcome every temptation, every habit, every sin, which seeks to destroy us, and instead of being under the mastery of that which seeks to destroy, we will come under the mastery of one who gives life and gives it in abundance, and for eternity.

The first Murder

Cain and his brother, Abel, both came to God, in order to worship and bring an offering. One came to worship, bringing his best, putting God first, the other came bringing what was left over and cost little. When the brother who brought the left overs to God, found neither he nor his gift were accepted, he became angry. Despite that response God chose to speak to Cain to try and help him do what was right and avoid his anger developing into something far worse.

A gap of time has now passed between verses seven and eight. How long has passed, we are not told, but in the intervening time Cain has stopped listening to what God is saying, and allowed the anger and jealousy to marinate in his heart. The unwillingness of Cain to listen to the voice of God and obey His word ultimately leads Cain to the events which now begin to unfold.

Cain comes to speak to his brother Abel. Having spoken we find the two brothers are together in the field. None of the conversation leading to them being in the field is included in the text. If you happen to see one of those Bible versions which gives any part of that conversation, you should know the words are the result of somebody making it up and adding it into the Bible. All the Hebrew text tells us is that 'Cain spoke to his brother Abel.'

The first murder is about to take place in the earth. It started like this, Cain spoke to Abel his brother. I wonder what he said. Did he speak about the worship they had engaged in? Did he just invite him to go on a walk and have a talk, as brothers, just to get to know each other and spend some time together? The conversation that took place is not recorded, but somehow Cain said to Abel, 'let's have a chat' and they are found together in the field.

Surely, we often think, there can be nothing wrong in talking. But actually it depends what is in the heart of the one who comes and just wants to talk. When someone says, "let's just talk about this" many times we discover, talking is not the intended aim. All too often, there is more going on when someone suggests that we should have a chat about something.

The two brothers began to talk and as they talked they walked. It can be easier to walk while talking and to talk while walking. The brothers talk and walk. What happens as they talk and walk is significant. As they walked and talked Cain brought his brother into the field.

The field was the area Cain was familiar with. He brought his brother to his turf. They walked into a place which was familiar to Cain and where Cain felt secure. It was Cain's environment. Cain controlled where they moved to. He selected the place where, in his own environment he would feel safe to attack his brother. All Abel did was go for a walk.

When the brothers arrived in the field, the verse says 'Cain rose up.' The way the Hebrew puts it suggests that having talked for a while these two brothers got to a place where their talking led them to touch one another. You are not told what went on, or how they finished up touching. Maybe Cain put his arm around him as they talk. Maybe Cain found Abel put his arm round him. We do not know, but what we do know is this. Having touched, Cain lifted himself to his full height and killed his younger brother.

He slew him. Having killed his brother there must be a further gap of time between verses eight and nine. We can say that, because the next thing we read is that Cain has moved on. It suggests Cain kills Abel, and then he walks away as though nothing had happened. It is implied that Cain buried Abel, because by verse nine we discover the blood of Abel is crying out from a place within the ground. It implies that Cain killed his brother and buried him in the ground of the field, thinking that if he hid his sin he could get away with it. After all, he was out in the field. Nobody saw what was going on, nobody knew what he was doing. Surely he could get away with it. This space in time between verses eight and nine suggests he killed his brother, and then went and got on with his life as though nothing has happened.

How often do we do something wrong and then hope nobody has realised what we have done, and we try to just get on with life as though nothing has happened because even though we know it is wrong we do not want to own up to it. Like his father, Cain hid, but this time he did not hide himself, he just thought to hide his actions. I wonder what took place when he went home that evening and his brother never turned up?

After a while God comes to talk to Cain. Cain has committed the first ever murder and the next thing we are told is God comes looking for Cain with the desire to talk to him. Where sin runs deep His grace runs deeper. Too often, we want to write people off, while God is still talking to them. We can even be tempted to write ourselves off, and fail to realise God is still talking to us despite all we have done and thought to hide.

Once again when God speaks to Cain, He starts by asking a question. When God asks a question, He does not do that because He is looking for information, it is not because He does not know the answer. God keeps asking questions because He is looking to reach out to us. He wants us to think about what we are doing, and to get us to think about our thoughts and actions in a way which means we are willing to acknowledge where we are at and what we have been, and sometimes still are, involved in. God speaks with the desire to help us to return to Him.

We do not know how long God waited, after Cain had killed and buried his brother, before He came to speak with Cain once more. Was the delay long enough for Cain to think he had got away with the murder? How ever long the delay, God now comes with the question for Cain to answer. God asks 'Where is Abel your brother?'

Once again we have to realise we do not know the tone or manner either of God's question or of Cain's response. All we are told is that Cain responded with words about the relationship he had with Abel.

Did Cain answer God's question in a way which meant no more than this: "How should I know, am I my brother's keeper?" Maybe the tone of Cain's answer was really suggesting something like this to God; "I don't know, I thought you were looking after him". It is also possible to read the reply as though he was saying: "What are you asking me for, he is nothing to do with me."

Which one of those tones of voice and attitude of heart you decide Cain was exhibiting as you read his response will change the way you feel about him. All of them are possible not just from the words in the English translation but also from the Hebrew text. We really do not know how Cain said the words, but the tone he used, changes the way you read and interpret his response to God.

It is quite reasonable to read it as though Cain was saying he thought God was the one who looked after them both. If you read it in that way, you may be inclined to believe Cain was making a declaration about his belief in the nature of God. It is just as allowable to read the words as though he was just excusing himself from the responsibility.

What we do know is this. However you read Cain's response and however you interpret the words he used, and wherever you put the emphasis on the words, Cain was refusing to own up to what he had done and what he knew had happened. The last thing any of us want to do is own up to how and when we mess up in life. That trait of our fallen humanity we recognise here in the response of Cain.

God was never going to leave it there. He is still wanting to reach out to Cain. Even as He had reached out before to both Adam and Eve. God now asks a second question. He comes and asks Cain, "What have you done?".

I want to suggest that God then stopped to give Cain a further opportunity to own his sin. I think that because it still seems obvious that God does not ask the question to get information. He already knew every detail of all Cain had done. He is trying to get Cain to own up to the mess he has got himself in. God came and said "What have you done?"

We always seem to think we can get away with our sin. It may even seem possible to hide it for so long we think it is buried and nobody knows. But God has seen and heard each thought and every intent of our hearts. He fully knows every action we have engaged in, and He comes and looks for each of us to own our sin for ourselves, and look to Him for His response to our admission of guilt.

With no reply from Cain to this question God moves on again. Now He explains He not only knows what has taken place, He is now ready to bring into the open all that Cain has done, where he has gone wrong, and the extent of the sin he has engaged in. God declares "the voice of your brother's blood is crying to me from the ground."

This is the first time we are told of anything Abel said! We know at least he went for a walk and he talked with his brother, but this is the first time Abel speaks. Then notice it is his blood which speaks. We are told blood has a voice which reaches the ear of the eternal God.

It is the first time 'blood' is mentioned in the Bible. Where it says the blood 'cried' the word in the Hebrew suggests that the blood was screaming out a loud plea in the ear of God.

Blood always speaks and blood always cries for justice. Abel's blood has raised it's voice to cry out for justice, for God to do that which is right in view of the blood which has been shed. Every time we come across blood within the scripture, we discover it has a voice, it always calls for God to do that which is right in view of the blood which has been shed and because of the reason for which it has been poured out. It is a first introduction to the power and voice of blood.

God comes to Cain and says the blood which you shed is still crying out at the top of it's voice for me to do the right thing, for me to bring justice to this situation you now find yourself in. God comes and explains to Cain that every sin, even if you think you have got away with it, will always bring a consequence into the existence of the one who sins.

Because Cain has sinned, he finds that God declares a curse which has come upon him. This is the first time a curse is ever pronounced against humanity. When Adam and Eve sinned, the serpent was cursed, the ground was cursed, childbirth was to be experienced with the addition of a curse. Now a curse is pronounced upon the activity of the one who has committed sin.

God here declares, 'there is a consequence to what has been done. You chose to commit sin, that will always bring a consequence, and the one who commits the sin has no choice about the nature or extent of the consequence. We may choose how we live, we may choose not to do right, but having made the choice we have to face the consequences whatever they are, they cannot be altered or avoided by us. The nature of the consequences of sin can never be chosen.

God comes and tells Cain that the curse which has come upon him because of his sin, has come out of the ground, out of the earth which received his brother, the one who Cain thought he had obliterated any memory of. He thought he had hidden his sin, he thought he had got away with the sin, but instead there is a curse coming from the very hiding place he had chosen to cover over his actions.

The nature of the curse is simple. Whenever Cain sought to work the soil, he would discover it failed to give of it's best. Then God adds the sin of Cain and his failure to admit his guilt would make him a fugitive and a wanderer in the earth.

The result of sin is twofold. First, this curse comes from the ground which will refuse to bring forth as it once had, the second result of his actions is that he will be unable to rest, unable to settle down in quietness and peace. He will always be running looking for and trying to discover a place to settle, but never able to find peace. Always looking for something and somewhere else. Cain was to become a wanderer, always bemoaning his lot in life.

Sin will always finish up doing that to us. It removes our peace, our ability to be settled in quiet rest and assurance, always looking for the next thing to satisfy, the next place to be settled, always unable to enter into a place of contentment and peace. Unable to settle down and just enjoy life. It leaves us feeling like the restless sea, always moving, and always changing. It makes us feel uncertain, unsure, with the desire to keep running away from the presence of God.

Cain responded to this assessment by God.
> *"My punishment is greater than I can bear. Behold, you have driven me today away from the ground, and from your face I shall be hidden. I shall be a fugitive and a wanderer on the earth, and whoever finds me will kill me."*
> *Genesis 4:13-14*

Once more we ought to understand these words of Cain can be translated and interpreted in two very different ways.

The critical words are "punishment" and "bear". It is possible to translate those words as they appear in the ESV and to read them with using a tone and placing the emphasis in a way which makes Cain say something like this: "I know I messed up, but God what you are saying is just not fair."

152

Reading it in that way makes Cain look as though he was wanting to argue with God and was trying to cut a better deal. Like that it suggests Cain thought God was being unfair. As an aside, we never want to be in a place where we argue with God about what is fair, with an aim of ensuring He deals with us in a fair way, or in a way which is based on what we deserve. I never want God to deal fairly with me. I never want Him to give me what I deserve.

The Hebrew word translated 'punishment' is a word which in other places is translated by the English word 'sin'. Sin and punishment share this Hebrew word. Then, the Hebrew word translated 'bear' is a word which in other places in the Bible is translated by the English word 'forgive'.

If you take those other translations, it is possible that when Cain spoke these words, instead of suggesting he was being dealt with harshly or unfairly, he was actually saying something like this; "God my sin is so great that you surely cannot forgive. I know I messed up really badly, and I know the result of what I did means things can never be put back to the way things were, because his body is there lying in the ground. I can never put it back, but is there no way for me to find forgiveness, no way for you to overlook my sin."

Reading it in that way, Cain is saying what many of us have found ourselves thinking. We sin, we mess up in life, we had not realised how far our sin would take us, and how extensive would be the consequences of that sin. We reach the place of wondering whether there is any way of ever being forgiven. "My punishment is more than I can hope to live with, my sin is so great, God have you cast me out forever."

Cain then says God has driven him away from the earth, and

away from God's face. He acknowledges he will become a wanderer and a fugitive on the face of the earth, and he fears that without God watching over him everyone and anyone who finds him will kill him.

> *Behold, you have driven me today away from the ground, and from your face I shall be hidden. I shall be a fugitive and a wanderer on the earth, and whoever finds me will kill me." Genesis 4:14*

Cain declares he has listened to God and now believes God is driving him away, not just from the ground, but also from His presence. But God never said that. He did say Cain would be a fugitive and a wanderer. He did say Cain was under a curse. But God never once said Cain would be driven away never to see the face, the favour of God again.

Sin makes us mishear what God says. Sin will make us think that the God of Heaven is against us. It will make us think that the God of Heaven is out to get us and God never says He is driving any away from Him without hope of ever seeing His favour again. But Cain was right in this sense. He declares "My greatest fear, the greatest punishment I could expect is never to see your face again, never to know your favour, never to find a way back and when I leave you God I know I am vulnerable, I am uncovered and anything could happen."

Despite all that Cain has done, God never left it at that, instead He speaks once more to Cain with the intention of giving him the beginnings of hope and comfort.

It is a hope and comfort we can all take, for all of us sin. Many of us have messed up really badly in life. The reality for many of us is, we wish we could go back and put some of it right, or even try better not to go so far from what we were meant to do and be, but it is water under the bridge. Satan will try to suggest that there is no way for us to come to God, and that God has given up on us. But God has never given up on us, any more than He was going to leave Cain entirely alone in the world.

God now tells Cain, He will put a mark on him. We may wonder what the mark was, but we are not told. We only know God put a mark on Cain. God told Cain He would mark him out so that wherever Cain went God would see him. Wherever he ran, God would still see him. Wherever he went God would still watch over him. Cain might think he was running from God and God had turned away and lost interest in him, but God told him, Cain could never run beyond His watchful care.

God effectively declares to Cain, He made him, and whatever he has done, he still belongs to his maker. God will never give up on watching out for him, watching over him and looking for him to turn again towards Him.

That is true for every one of us born on the face of this earth. It is why the psalmist years later would record,

> *Where shall I flee from your presence? If I ascend to heaven, you are there! If I make my bed in Sheol, you are there! If I take the wings of the morning and dwell in the uttermost parts of the sea, even there your hand shall lead me, and your right hand shall hold me. If I say, "Surely the darkness shall cover me, and the light about me be night," even the darkness is not dark to you; the night is bright as the day, for darkness is as light with you. For you formed my inward parts; you*

> *knitted me together in my mother's womb.*
> *Psalm 139:7-13*

His grace will find us no matter how far we have messed up. God says there is some bad news, but there is also some good news. The bad news is, there are consequences to the mess we make, the sin we engage in. We will have to go through some consequences. The good news is there are consequences to the mess we make, the sin we engage in, and even though there are consequences we face, God says not only does He mark us out He will still watch out for us and look out for us, longing for us to turn back to Him to seek and find a restored relationship with Him.

Moreover any thing or anyone that tries to damage, to steal, to kill, or to destroy us, God promises He will destroy them. The enemy can form weapons against us, but they will never be able to take us so far from God's gaze that God's hand will not be there for us, and His heart still cares for us and longs for us to return to Him.

I don't know how many times you have read or listened to people explaining this portion in Genesis as though it is a condemnatory word, but truly that is not the main thrust of this portion. Instead it is to be read as a message of hope that, wherever we are, whatever we have done, however far we may have wandered, whatever mess our lives seem to be in, God's presence, His watch and His care is still there for us, and He still waits for us to turn back to Him and discover His love.

Understand there is nothing worth more than His presence. In life never keep running from God, let us always run towards Him own the mess we have made and the sin we have engaged in, and we will find His arms of mercy and grace reaching out to embrace us. We will never find peace away from him. But in His presence, there is forgiveness, there is fullness of joy and there are pleasures for ever more.

Legacies from Eden

From the very first word of Genesis, God has been revealing Himself and His eternal plan of creation and salvation. He has shown something of His majesty and glory, something about the founding of the creation. We have seen something about the way God placed the first humans in the Eden, in a garden that was a place of paradise. It was made a paradise by the closeness of the presence of the living God. His presence will make anywhere different. His presence will bring a taste of what Eden was like, and what heaven will always be like.

Having spoken of those first humans God's plan for them to be incomplete unless they enjoyed a relationship with God and with one another has been revealed. Man placed in the paradise of God's presence chose to act in defiance and disobedience was then excluded from Eden, driven out and travelling eastwards. Having left Eden moving eastwards the first siblings enter the world. Out of jealousy, and envy grew hatred, and then murder. Having slain his brother, Cain moves further from Eden. He went out from the presence of the Lord travelling further and further from the known experience of the presence of God. All the while wandering in sin mankind is moving yet further eastward.

As we read these verses it is important to recognise that moving eastwards is symbolic of walking away from the recognition and enjoyment of the presence of the living God. That does not mean if we travel to the east today, we are automatically going further away from God, but this easterly travel is symbolic both here and throughout the Scriptures. If we grasp that symbolism we will understand so much more of the underlying shadows as we read through the rest of the

Scripture. For example, it can helps us understand why on His way into Jerusalem, on that last journey before the cross, Jesus came in from the east. It will help us realise why when he carried our sins to the cross, we are told He walked out of the east gate. It will bring meaning to His Second Coming which once more sees Him coming back to set all things right, travelling into the city through the eastern gate. In all of those references, Jesus is to be seen bringing a people back into the enjoyment of the presence of the living God which they had once fled from. Because going east, is symbolic of wandering from the presence of God, coming back from the east is symbolic of restoration and return.

As Cain journeys away from God, he is wandering from three things. He is leaving behind the favour of the land closest to Eden. God told him in wandering life is going to get more difficult. God said, as he goes, he will face more struggles, which he will not know how to handle. Cain is wandering into a world where he will face struggles that he does not know how to deal with.

Then, he is wandering from the face of God. Throughout the scriptures the face of God speaks of the smile and favourable presence of the Lord. When Cain decides to walk away from the face of God he is choosing to turn his back on God, and walk in direct variance to the favour and ways of God.

He is also choosing to wander away from his family and his home. We discover he does not leave on his own, he is going with his wife. But he is leaving the home of his parents, he is leaving the place where he heard about God. He chooses to wander from God takes his wife with him, for in wandering, he wants to take somebody with him.

He now wanders away from those three blessings in life. He leaves, and he is going to dwell in the land of Nod on the east. He is intentionally continuing the journey eastward and makes his way to the land of Nod.

The land of Nod does not speak of any particular place, but Nod is significant for us to grasp. The Hebrew word 'Nod' speaks less of a particular place and more of a moving area. It is a word which means wandering. It speaks of wandering aimlessly, of moving without knowing the final destination of your journey. It tells us Cain is leaving the favour of the land, the face of God, the blessings of family and home, and is journeying, with no idea of any particular destination. He is wandering into a place of further wandering. He is roaming further and further eastward, further and further from fellowship with God.

People are ever the same. Something happens that upsets them. They used to be in the centre of the will of God, but something happens, and they slowly move further and further from the blessing and favour of God. They start walking from the favour of where they once dwelt, turning their backs on the face of God and desiring to have less to do with the family of God and the house of God. Their real problem is always about a spiritual condition. It is always about their relationship and God.

Cain began to wander, and as he wanders we see the first family being destroyed. When we wander from fellowship with God it is not long before a family is broken up.

> *Cain knew his wife, and she conceived and bore*
> *Enoch. When he built a city, he called the name of*
> *the city after the name of his son, Enoch.*
> *Genesis 4:17*

161

This is not the Enoch we read about who walked with God. This is a different Enoch. Cain had a son who he called Enoch, and then he built a city and called the name of the city by his son's name.

The text does not tell us how long Cain wandered before building the city. We can guess it was at least nine months, because he does not settle down until his first son is born. How far may he have wandered from God in those months of being always on the move.

The text does tell us that as he wandered from God things continued to change in his heart and life. In wandering Cain has continued to feel more and more unsettled and unsafe. We can tell that because with the arrival of the boy he stops and builds a city. It would have been more difficult to keep wandering with a new baby, but that is not the clue to the mentality of Cain at this stage.

It says he built a city. There are a number of Hebrew words that are translated 'city'. This one has less to do with the size of the place, than the construction. In recording the building of a city, there is no clue whether it was a big place or a little place. It could have been a single house and still use this word 'city' for this word speaks of a fortified and secure dwelling.

What we are being told seems to be that Cain found himself unable to keep moving because of what has happened in his life with the birth of a baby, but when he stopped wandering he felt so unsafe, he needed to build a secure wall around him and add a covering, a roof, over the place which he built to live in. Having continued to walk further and further from the awareness of God's protection and covering he felt insecure. Certainly he was settling down, in terms of living in the same place, but every moment he is there, he wonders what is going on around him, and who may be coming after him to do him harm.

He was not dwelling in an area with crowds of people. The world is still not heavily populated, yet he felt a deep need in his heart. A need for a wall of protection around him and some kind of covering over his life.

The more we wander from living in fellowship with God the more we can feel the need to do something to secure our safety. When we walk in the certainty of our relationship with the living God we know what it is to dwell within His wall of protection. His protection surrounds us, wherever we go, and what ever happens, we are covered by the blood of Jesus the Christ.

> *The angel of the Lord encamps around those who*
> *fear him, and delivers them. Oh, taste and see that*
> *the Lord is good! Blessed is the man who takes*
> *refuge in him!*   *Psalm 34:7-8*

Cain felt unsafe and unsure of everything in a world where there was only him and his wife.

Just as an aside, some ask where his wife came from? The next chapter in Genesis tells us Adam and Eve had other sons and daughters. It seems he married his sister. We do not do that today, but when there was nobody else around it would have been the only way for the first couple to fill the world.

After Cain built the city, in time, Enoch grew up and had a son, and his son had a son and so the genealogy continues with little comment until seven generations on from Adam, a man called Lamech was born.

> *To Enoch was born Irad, and Irad fathered*
> *Mehujael, and Mehujael fathered Methushael,*
> *and Methushael fathered Lamech. And Lamech*
> *took two wives. The name of the one was Adah,*
> *and the name of the other Zillah. Adah bore Jabal;*
> *he was the father of those who dwell in tents and*
> *have livestock. His brother's name was Jubal; he*
> *was the father of all those who play the lyre and*
> *pipe. Zillah also bore Tubal-cain; he was the*
> *forger of all instruments of bronze and iron. The*
> *sister of Tubal-cain was Naamah. Lamech said to*
> *his wives: "Adah and Zillah, hear my voice; you*
> *wives of Lamech, listen to what I say: I have killed*
> *a man for wounding me, a young man for striking*
> *me. If Cain's revenge is sevenfold, then Lamech's*
> *is seventy-sevenfold."*   *Genesis 4 18-24*

Every so often in the biblical genealogies there is a
commentary on one of the names, an expansion of detail,
which is always significant to the reader. In the arrival of
Lamech, there is just such an addition. It stands there to show
the natural legacy which comes from walking away from a
vital relationship with God.

We need to see that Lamech is the seventh generation of this
family who walked further and further away from the
paradise of God's favour and smile. Seven is the number of
completeness. Actually Lamech will have a son who will be
the end of the line. Cain's line is about to die out.

Six generations of Cain's family who wandered away from
the favour of the land, the smile of God's face and the family
around them, and Lamech is born. Lamech took to himself
two wives. It started when Cain walked away from the family

unit that God had set in place. Now, as Cain has wandered further, into a place of insecurity, and fear, his descendants will, for the first time, start the practice of polygamy.

The descendants of Cain are going to corrupt God's whole plan for marriage and family life. God's plan for marriage and the family was the man should never be on his own. On his own, man is incomplete and flawed. The man needs a woman. That was and still is God's plan. It was God's creation ordinance. It is the covenant that God set down at the beginning. It is a sacred covenant, one man and one woman. It is ever God's ideal for humanity. We should never lose sight of that. It is why marriage and the family is under so great an attack in our world.

Lamech, took two wives. It means that he found a woman who wanted a man so much she was prepared to share him with another woman. She was so desperate she settled with a man who was already with someone else. It is part of the legacy of Cain. It sets out to destroy the family, and corrupt God's whole plan for life.

Lamech decided he was so great one wife could not satisfy him. What made him feel the need for more than one? How did this arrangement work, for either wife?

Today, the world system is promoting a way of life with easy relationships, extra marital affairs, family breakdowns, corruption of one man with one woman, and all of it is being portrayed as though it is 'normal'. It is all in direct opposition to the revealed word of God, and against the creation ordinances of God. It is in contradiction to the plan and purpose of God, and it's aim is to take the world further and further into a place of fear, wandering aimlessly away from

God until nobody will remember God's original plan and purpose to bless humanity as they chose to live their lives within the boundaries and guidelines He has set down.

When Lamech took two wives, he was not only corrupting the plan of God he was abusing the covenant relationship within marriage. It became the first episode of family abuse.

Lamech said to his two wives, 'hear my voice I killed somebody who hurt me?' The tone of this and the way it is translated suggests Lamech told them both with a sense of arrogance and pride that somebody had hit him, so he had got them back by killing them. His attitude is one of brutality and belligerence. If you hurt him, if you hit him his response is to kill you. Life, to Lamech, has become cheap.

The sacred life which God gave into this world sees the destruction of a family the overturning of the marriage covenant, abuse within the family life and violence and murder, cheapening life for any who stand in the way of selfish and abusive people.

The murder Lamech committed was something he was proud to boast of. He had slain a young man. He killed someone who must have been related to him, through the six generations from Cain. He kills, without any sense of remorse or shame. His conscience is so seared, he can boast of doing what his ancestor did. Cain had tried to hide his sin, but to Lamech, his sin has reached the place where it is something to boast of. He kills, believes he can get away with it and then adds, if anyone tries to stop him the revenge he will reek will be ten times worse than any vengeance Cain may have depended on.

166

Paul puts the end result of living without God in this way;

> *filled with all manner of unrighteousness, evil, covetousness, malice. They are full of envy, murder, strife, deceit, maliciousness. They are gossips, slanderers, haters of God, insolent, haughty, boastful, inventors of evil, disobedient to parents, foolish, faithless, heartless, ruthless. Though they know God's righteous decree that those who practice such things deserve to die, they not only do them but give approval to those who practice them.* Romans 1:29-32

It all started when Cain turned his back on God and began to wander from any fellowship with God. It stands as a signpost to us. We chose to wander from God and His ways at our peril. Our wandering will take its toll not only on us but often on our children for the generations that follow.

But, thank the living God, that is not the end of the story. It will be the end of Cain's descendents. Yet in the midst of all of Cain's story and legacy of wandering away from God, God still has a plan.

Eve has lost one son who has been killed. She has then lost a second son and a daughter who have wandered far away. But she and Adam have stayed in the vicinity of the presence of God, and their story is picked up again, if only briefly, yet with the light of hope shining from the words.

> *And Adam knew his wife again, and she bore a son and called his name Seth, for she said, "God has appointed for me another offspring instead of Abel, for Cain killed him."* Genesis 4:25

A replacement son is born. It appears from the text that this was the next boy Eve gives birth to. She calls him Seth. The name comes from a Hebrew word which speaks of 'a substitute'. Eve said, "I lost the one that I thought God had his hand on. I am still close by to paradise, just on the east of Eden, and God has given me another son. I am going to call this new boy, Seth."

Choosing to call him Seth or 'substitute', suggests that she is still holding on to God's promise of a seed who will come and deal with all that had gone wrong. She holds on to this thought that God has replaced Abel, giving her a live son, as a substitute for the one killed by Cain. She had waited for the promise to come that would solve the problem of the sin she and her husband had committed, which had led to them being driven out of the garden. She realised Cain could not be the seed, Abel was dead but holding on to the promise she declares she has a substitute. He may have been born and be living on the east side, but living there among sinners she saw a new and living hope.

As far as we can tell, Cain was never spoken about again. As far as we can tell, Cain never spoke about his sin again. So often when there is abuse and violence in a family, it is hidden away, never to be mentioned, never to be spoken of, even though the ramifications of it run through the years, and the generations.

Leaving the generations of Cain, the story takes on new hope in Seth. In time this substitute has a son and he calls his name Enosh. That name speaks of mankind. The substitute has a son, calls him mankind, a new ancestral descent, and from that time men began to call on the name of Jehovah God, the living God, the God who is all I need Him to be.

To Seth also a son was born, and he called his

> *name Enosh. At that time people began to call*
> *upon the name of the LORD.*   *Genesis 4:26*

That word "call" means to call out, to speak, to call on, and to shout out to. It is a word that will run all the way through the Bible narrative. Eventually in the Scriptures, it is a word which will be used for giving praise and adoration.

There outside of Eden, on the east side, but not too far away, close enough to be where you could remember the fellowship once enjoyed, close enough to be in the vicinity of God's favour and smile, close enough to not feel the need to run and hide, God gave a substitute. Then when the substitute came people began to worship and shout out their praises to God.

Eve had a son, and Seth has a son, and that son had a son, and that line continued down through the Bible until one day, we arrive at the birth of Jesus the Christ. As soon as the substitute was born, men began to call out to the living God in worship and praise. They stopped wandering east and began to turn round. Some may have travelled way, way out to the east far away from God, but they began to turn around, to turn back and call out in hope, as an expression of worship and praise to God.

That word 'east' is an interesting word. We said earlier, it speaks symbolically of travelling away from a place of knowing God. But the same Hebrew root word in this word 'East' is also a word from which comes the concept of 'a new beginning'.

In the east, having wandered from knowing God, mankind began to turn around and look once more towards where the presence of God had been known and where His favour and smile had been lost sight of. There they began to call out to God. They needed a substitute, one who would fulfil the promise to crush the head of the serpent. As they call out God declares it to be a day of new beginnings. Because no matter how far we wander, no matter how far we have gone, no matter how bad we think our situation is, no matter how much we have lived outside of the will and ways of God, when we call on the name of the Lord the eternal God, He is still able to give each of us a new beginning.

That root word became known for new beginnings because it spoke of the east, and it is in the east where the sun rises. Whoever will turn to God and call out to him in worship will discover not only does the sun rise in the east, but there far from God, ensnared by sin and failure, far from where God intended us to be we can still experience the Son rising again, on our heart and soul.

This book of beginnings, is a book about the mess our ancestors made. It is about the mess we all make. But, even more than that it is a book which speaks of new beginnings and new hope. It speaks of a substitute who will take our place, and shed His blood, blood which will cry to God, crying out not of vengeance, but of justice, of an innocent dying in our place, pleading for justice which cannot condemn again those who have called out and trusted in God's substitute who died in our place.

As we turn our face towards Him we see His smile is still there for us, His arms are yet outstretched to welcome us back. He can deal with our guilt. He can mend our brokenness. He can deal with the abuse we have gone through. He can deal with the violence we have been subjected to, and He can deal with the pain of our heart. More than all of that He is able to give us a new beginning, a beginning which will remove our fear, disperse our shame and bring us to a place of enjoyment in the presence and favour of the living God.

My hope and prayer is, that all who have read their way through these pages will find their way to following the example of the descendants of Seth and call upon the name of the God of heaven, made known to us in Jesus the Christ and revealed to us by God the Holy Spirit.

Annex

*There follow verses written by the author
at an earlier period in life.
They are included with the hope and prayer they
may be used by the reader to aid their personal
devotions and prayerful engagement with the
triune God.*

They appear in no particular order.

The Word of the Father
Based on Hebrews 1

See and ponder, God's great mercy
In the giving of His Son.
Meditate upon the mystery
Of the dying Holy One.
Hear the Father's final message
In the person of His Son;
Purging all sin's deepest staining.
Mighty victory is won!

Kneel before the foot of Calvary
See the blood so freely shed.
Precious wounds of Christ, my Saviour
Crown of thorn upon His head.
Dying there, He makes the payment
That was due for all my sin.
Blood of Jesus, Blood most precious;
Shed that I might be made clean.

Oh what mystery! The eternal
God should die; upon the tree.
Greater mystery; consider,
Dies for love of you and me.
Here death has it's final death blow
Satan's head is crushed and bruised,
In the Saviour, sin is dealt with.
Hear salvation's wondrous news.

The day of His coming
Based on Malachi 3

Who may abide, when He is come,
Or who that day shall stand?
For He appears with holy truth
And power in His hand:
To purify, refine and purge
The dross, within His own;
To pour His wrath on all who stand
Against His righteous throne.

When many least expect, behold
He comes so suddenly.
Too late, too late, to think again
Or change your destiny.
On all, He says, who fear Him not,
He'll bring swift judgement sure.
Oh stir my soul, before that time
His being to adore.

Help me to fear you, mighty God
With righteous, holy fear;
My sin to know – your grace to feel;
Your love to me make clear.
Before that great and awful day
Refine away my sin.
Come now, yourself, to this poor heart
O love, reside within.

I love Him, because he first loved me

O Triune Majesty, who dwells in light,
Beyond the reach of my poor sinful sight,
Whose ways are higher than the thought of man;
I bring my praise for your eternal plan.

>I love the Lord, because He first loved me.
>I love the Son, who died on Calvary.
>I love the Spirit who made known to me
>The love of Christ, who died to set me free.

And when in time the hour had fully come,
Under the law, God sent His only Son.
Born of a virgin, to remove the curse.
He died the death appointed unto us.

While of myself my eyes could never see;
The gospel truth that saves eternally.
The silent work is done so deep within;
To free my life from death, my soul from sin.

Thus has the Spirit brought about the work
Available, because the Son did shirk
Not from the Cross, nor from the Father's plan
For reconciling God with sinful man

This . . . done for you

See now once more, the table spread for me;
That speaks with accents clear of Calvary.
The wondrous gift of Christ, the Son of God;
Who gave himself and shed His precious blood.

Behold the bread, within the Saviour's hands,
And hear the word He utters to His friends:
'This is my body, broken now for you:
Take, eat' – believe, and all His way pursue.

Give me, O Lord, the broken, contrite heart.
Bend me and mould me, mighty as Thou art.
Let holy brokenness be ever mine;
Despise me not – accept me now as Thine.

'Here is the cup of the new testament,
Shed for my people', thus the Father sent
Into the world His best beloved Son
To pour His life blood. Mercy's work is done.

So let my soul be all poured out for Thee
In sacrifice to one whose love was free.
Reflect in me the fragrance of the Lord.
Within my heart be Thou, O Lamb adored.

Yea, He is altogether lovely

Thy blood, O Christ my Saviour,
Is now my only plea.
All other hopes are failure,
I cling by faith to Thee.
Sin in my life had flourished;
My heart all vile had been.
But now, Thy love has ravished
Thy grace my eyes have seen.

My eyes now gaze upon Him,
His beauty I adore.
His cross, by faith, I cling to
E'er since this love I saw.
The fairest of ten thousand
His person to my soul.
He, altogether lovely,
Has made this sinner whole.

I sing the praise of Jesus;
His person thrills my soul,
The wonder of His beauty;
The grace that made me whole.
Oh heart, rejoice with fervour:
Upon His beauty gaze.
Make known His name for ever
My lips repeat His praise.

Triune Majesty

Immeasurable splendour
Belongs to God on high.
The greatness of His glory
Defines infinity.
Unbounded is this being;
Adored by hosts above.
In whom alone the living
Can live, and breathe and move.

Incomparable sweetness
The Father's greatest Word.
Ineffable the beauty
That's found in Christ the Lord.
He is the satisfaction
Of every living soul.
The bruised and broken hearted
He, only, can make whole.

Insuperable Mercy
Which God the Spirit brings.
Intangible His working;
Yet in my spirit sings
That one new song of glory
And praise to God most high.
The evidence of pardon
And life eternally.

Near to His heart

There is a place, where I may stay
And shelter from the heat of day:
      'Neath the Almighty's wing.
And 'though around, the battle's hot
To bring despair – the tempter's plot:
      Here still I rest and sing.

'By my own name. By my own Word,'
In this He does my hope record,
      And shall I ever fear.
For here's an anchor for my soul,
Salvation's cleansing free and whole:
      His love has drawn me near.

His Spirit, pure, will intercede,
In cries more strong than I can plead
      To lift my soul above.
His promise is so strong and sure,
It reaches me, though weak and poor:
      Embracing me in love

All gracious God to Thee I bow –
Your love hath conquered in me now;
      O never let me roam!
For here I would each day abide;
And deeper in Thy love would hide
      Until I reach my home.

Salvation's plan
Based on 2 Corinthians 5:21

Decides the triune God
    Before the world began.
To send to earth the Word;
    Love's mighty grace and plan.
God's holy Son to earth comes down
And lays aside His throne and crown.

The Son of Glory, see,
    Becomes a perfect man,
To keep God's holy law
    Fulfilling each command.
Tempted was He, yet without sin.
His righteousness to me is given.

His life will not suffice,
    To take away my sin.
Death is the law's full price
    For all that I have done.
He dies, and by His blood my sin,
Is washed away, my soul made clean.

Jesus my Lord and God
    The Saviour of my heart;
My soul shall Thee adore,
    The mighty God Thou art.
All glory now to Thee, my Lord;
Acclaimed by heaven with sweet accord.

Revive Thy Church
based on Isaiah 62

Lord, look down, from heaven your dwelling,
On this weary sin-sick land.
View your Church in such confusion;
Can this be what you had planned.

> Favour you have shown before this
> On our broken ruined land.
> Mercy greater than the heavens
> From a heart supremely kind.

Hear the cry within your remnant,
Hear this prayer which comes from me.
Turn your wrath from our condition,
All our barrenness now see.

Raise yourself, O God in heaven,
From your habitation come.
Stir yourself, lift high the standard.
Make the Church your glorious crown.

If you will not come in person,
Can we still believe your Word.
For 'Your Church cannot be beaten',
You have said it, Sovereign Lord.

Come, oh come, revive your people
Satisfy this awful thirst.
Once again this barren desert;
Into fragrant blossom burst.

'Give heaven no rest'

Raise up the name of Jesus
His glory magnify.
Rebuild the broken highways
Though ruined long they lie.
You watchmen on the towers
Give heaven no time of peace;
But cry to God Almighty
His kingdom to increase.

Raise up the name of Jesus;
My Saviour, God and Lord.
Restore the royal kingdom,
Make known the living Word;
That every town and village,
Each home and family,
May know His mighty power
Saving eternally.

Raise up the name of Jesus;
Whose reign shall know no end.
Come down, oh promised blessing
Thy peace o'er all extend.
Let malice, lies and envy
No more afflict our race;
But let this earth experience
Our God's redeeming grace.

Miracle of Grace

Amazing miracle Divine
That God should come to me
That I might know that 'He is mine',
No more from Him need flee.

In Christ, the Lord will reconcile
My guilty soul to Him.
My heart, my mind, so very vile,
By Him is all forgiven.

The old the wicked and the bad
All, all is passed away –
In Christ, I need no more be sad
But new, be made, this day.

For he has made His blessed Son
The bearer of my sin;
And me, the guilty, sinful, one:
God's righteousness in Him.

Then keep my eyes all fixed on Him
Your love my soul o'erflow.
With God made one – His praise to sing
His precious presence know.

He is altogether lovely

Precious Jesus; Son of God,
Came to shed his mighty blood:
Came to pay the awful cost
To redeem us, sinners, lost.

Fragrance of the valleys flower,
Barren deserts needful shower;
Great salvation, see He brings,
Mighty healing in His wings!

Brightness of the Father's face
King of Glory, full of grace,
Leaves the Majesty on high,
Ruined sinners – come – draw nigh!

Gaze upon the morning star;
Stay no more from God afar,
Wash you in the Saviour's blood
Cleanse you, in the heavenly flood.

All your sins then washed away
Stand redeemed in Christ today.
Bring your worship, love and praise
Unto God, for mercy's ways.

The valley of deep darkness

I walked in the vale of dark shadows
Where trials and problems o'erflow,
Yet when I am sinking in sorrows
While round me the fierce winds do blow
There's one, who with me ever goeth
A shepherd who feels every woe
My weakness and trouble He knoweth
To me then, His love, He doth show.

I hear whispered doubts and despairing
But I know my Saviour still cares;
And when my heart seems close to tearing
I know He will answer my prayers.
Though briefly the clouds are displaying
Their darkness, I need have no fears.
His Word tells me glory is waiting;
And there He will dry all my tears.

Though evil now plots to destroy me
My God shall o'erule, and I'll see
In all things He is great and mighty,
Jehovah thrice holy is He.
My God's on the throne in the glory,
He rules o'er the land, and the sea,
His purpose, He'll work out supremely;
And this God thinks peace towards me.

Why then shall I fear for the morrow
Since my God plans all from His throne,
He brings from each trial and sorrow,
A beauty that He loves to own.
He turns me from earth's joy, so hollow,
He nurtures the seed He has sown
He helps me the Saviour to follow,
'Til I cast before Him my crown

Will He still know us (based on Isaiah 63)

Where is He that bought His people
Out of Egypt through the sea.
Put His Holy Spirit on them
Caused their enemies to flee?
Our rebellion vexed your Spirit
Causing you to turn away.
Wilt you not look down from heaven
Turn us back to you today?

Should the saints of old look on us
Could they recognise your grace?
But you know, O righteous Father
On us shine your lovely face.
We are yours; O stay not from us!
Show your zeal, display your strength:
Cause your fear our hearts to soften,
Turn us back to you at length.

All the sanctuary lies trodden
'Neath our adversaries feet.
Our own sin, has brought this on us,
Yet we come before your seat.
There to plead the promised blessings
Everlasting is your name.
In your mercy, for your glory,
Turn us back to you again.

Rend the heavens, melt the mountains
Of resistance in my heart.
Come yourself in power and beauty
Lord of all my hope you are.
Make us tremble at your power,
Make us wonder at your love.
By your presence, move our spirits;
Turn us Father from above.

He will keep me!

In the midst of tribulation
Doubts and fears within;
Still with me is power supernal,
Christ will win

Words and deeds of persecution
Fanning flames of hate;
But around – see angel forces
Victors yet!

All about is great confusion,
Fighting for my soul;
Might and clarity divine shall
Keep me whole.

Nothing now can e'er o'ertake me,
He, His word will keep.
God shall hold, and hold for ever
Me, His sheep.

Thus will I rejoice through weakness;
Heart, mind, will, shall be
Kept secure, by the Almighty
One in Three

Think on these things

Lord Jesus, Saviour, Mighty Christ the Lord;
In Thee Alone is found the truthful Word
Thou art the source, for only here, in Thee
Is found the matchless truth that saveth me.

In all Thy dealings with my sinful soul;
Honour and justice meet to make me whole.
Holy art Thou, and yet it pleaseth Thee
To bear my sin and guilt upon the tree.

Fairer than all, Thou morning star, so bright
Thy beauty shines with never fading light.
Thou, Rose of Sharon, fragrance ever sweet;
Within my soul now burn, Thy love's pure heat.

Virtue and praise in Thee is ever found.
Peace comes to worry in that sweetest sound
Of Thy great name, Oh lover of my soul.
Reside within this heart, my all in all.

Go in and possess the land

"This land is ours" thus God hath said.
Come now the promise sue.
In all our ways, His grace has led,
His word is ever true.

This land is ours – How can we lie
In awful dark dismay?
Since God is ours, He'll hear our cry,
The weakest saint can pray.

This land is ours – Why shall we fear?
The victory is ours!
Our glorious God, His arm makes bear,
To manifest His powers.

This land is ours – Who then may doubt
Or turn from God away?
His arm will drive the tempter out,
His strength will win the day.

This land is ours – then in His might
Go forth to overcome.
So may the Gospel's glorious light
Find here a welcome home.

Come to me, O my beloved

The day, O Lord, is now far spent
And shadows lengthen fast;
Yet even in the deepest night
The blackness soon is past.

But even in the darkest hour
My cry ascends to Thee;
Turn back, O my beloved one
And stay awhile with me.

The sorrows far too long endure,
To greatly cloud my way.
My troubled, long divided heart
Now longs for Thee to stay.

Come quickly as a hart upon
These mountains that divide;
And lift my soul within the veil
There close with Thee reside.

There would I stay 'til dawn shall break
Upon eternal day;
Where shadows all are fled and gone
And night has passed away

'Give Him no rest'

Come down among us heavenly Dove,
Baptise us with Thy mighty love.
Help us, that we Thy word might hear,
And point us to a Saviour Dear

Take from our eyes the scales of sin.
Send forth Thy light our hearts within
The darkness of our souls bid flee
And give us grace to worship Thee.

Point us; from sin's dark realm away.
Point us; to see the coming day.
Grant us to know the Living Word,
Secure in Him, our Friend, our Lord.

Endue us with Thy mighty power,
Assurance give us in this hour.
So thus may many souls be reached
Whene'er Thy holy Word is preached.

O let the heavenly dew descend
The holy showers upon us send.
The name of Jesus magnify,
'Til all to Him for refuge fly.

The place of safety

My God, is any place as sweet
As where I seek Thy face.
Before Thy throne, beneath Thy feet
I find Thy matchless grace.

Thine eyes perpetually see;
Thine ears, my cry still hear;
Thy heart is open now to me;
Within the place of prayer.

Thy Word has bidden me 'draw nigh';
Thy Son has paved the way:
Thy Spirit uttering 'a sigh'
All help me as I pray.

Come then, and answer my desire,
That I with Thee might live.
Baptise me with Thy holy fire,
Thy gracious presence give.

Cause me to know that wondrous love,
And see the answer given.
Stay now with me, that here on earth,
Thy peace may be my heaven

Psalm 121

From whence shall our salvation come,
From God alone, who made all things.
He only is the eternal one;
The Lord of lords the King of kings.
He'll not allow your foot to move,
Nor can you slip, or fall from Him.
In each condition He will prove
His love for you can know no end.

See how His care for you extends,
Neither through day or night He fails
To watch on those He calls His friends,
Saved by Christ's blood, His care prevails.
He never slumbers, never sleeps,
His eyes they weary not nor rest.
His watch, through all your life He keeps
Working for you the will that's best.

Whilst o'er your soul His watch is sure,
Sun, moon, nor all that would molest
Can enter in to smite your soul
Or take from you His perfect rest.
While all the darkest host would smite
To bring you down and fill with fear.
He is your shade, and by His might
You are secure, your cry He'll hear.

He will, your going out preserve
Even into the darkest night.
He will, your coming in preserve
Into the brightness of His light.
Not only in this vale of tears,
But as you enter home at last
His arms surround you with His care
'Til all that harms forever's past.

Saved by God

Saved by grace! For life eternal
By our God whose power supernal
Reaching down from heaven's glory
Saved my soul. O wondrous story

Saved by faith of mercy given
Holy Spirit's mighty moving.
Veil of unbelief thus rending
Gospel light from heaven sending.

Saved by blood! The gift most gracious
Blood of Christ most efficacious.
Washing from sin's deepest staining
Hell's rejection: Heaven claiming!

Saved then marvel! Saved for ever
Glory to the triune splendour.
Soul thus praise, no more forsaken!
Unto God give adoration.